Writing 45-Minute One-Act Plays, Skits, Monologues, & Animation Scripts for Drama Workshops

Writing 45-Minute One-Act Plays, Skits, Monologues, & Animation Scripts for Drama Workshops

Adapting Current Events, Social Issues, Life Stories, News & Histories

Anne Hart

ASJA Press
New York Lincoln Shanghai

Writing 45-Minute One-Act Plays, Skits, Monologues, & Animation
Scripts for Drama Workshops
Adapting Current Events, Social Issues, Life Stories, News & Histories

ASJA Press
an imprint of iUniverse, Inc.

iUniverse books may be ordered through booksellers or by contacting:

iUniverse
2021 Pine Lake Road, Suite 100
Lincoln, NE 68512
www.iuniverse.com
1-800-Authors (1-800-288-4677)

ISBN: 0-595-34597-2

Printed in the United States of America

Contents

Introduction

Put *direct experience* in a small package. Dramatize and launch significant events worldwide with one-act plays, skits, monologues, narrations, anecdotes, or vignettes suitable for drama groups or classes *of all ages.* First write your life story or the highlights of current events and social issues in short vignettes of 1,500 to 1,800 words. For historical plays, research one event in the life of your main character and expand based on the experience of that particular time in history using social issues.

Then expand the vignette into a skit, play, or monologue. You can also uses the techniques for writing eulogies and anecdotes or vignettes of life stories, current events, social issues, and personal histories for mini-biographies and autobiographies. Then condense or contract the life stories or personal histories into PowerPoint presentations and similar slide shows on disks using lots of photos and one-page of life story.

Finally, collect lots of vignettes and flesh-out the vignettes, linking them together into first-person diary-style novels and books, plays, skits, or other larger works. Write memoirs or eulogies for people or ghostwrite biographies and autobiographies for others.

If ghostwriting is too invisible, write biographies and vocational biographies, success stories and case histories, and customize for niche interest groups. Your main goal with personal history and life stories is to take the direct experience itself and package each story as a vignette.

The vignette can be read in ten minutes. So fill magazine space with a direct experience vignette. Magazine space needs only 1,500 words. When you link many vignettes together, each forms a book chapter or can be adapted to a play or script.

By turning vignettes into one-act plays or monologues, you learn to condense social issues into packages. One-act plays run about 45 minutes and require around 45 pages of writing. A play usually runs a page per minute of action and speech. Short plays for a teenage acting crew are easier to launch to the media.

When collected and linked together, one-act plays suitable for high-school performances are expanded from a chain of vignettes offering nourishment, direction, purpose, and information used by people who need to make choices. Here's how to write those inspiration-driven, persistence-driven life plays, skits, and monologues taken from vignettes and what to do with them. Use universal experience with which we all can identify.

Included are a full-length diary-format first person novel and a three-act play, including a monologue for performances. There's a demand for direct life experiences written or produced as vignettes and presented in small packages. The enclosed play is in three acts. You can perform each act separately as a one-act play.

Save those vignettes electronically. Later, they can be placed together as acts in a play or chapters in a book. Write in easy-to read packages. First write the vignette of about 1,500 words. Then write the monologue. Expand the monologue into a one-act play. If there are significant experiences to include, it's better to have three one-act plays than one, long three-act play. Break the three-act play included in this book into three one-act plays and practice writing, revising, and if you desire, at no cost to me, performing the plays.

What you'll get out of this book and the exercises of writing one-act plays for teenagers or older adults, and audiences of any ages, are improved skills in adapting all types of social issues, current events, or significant life experiences to 45-minute one-act plays for your teenage or older adult drama workshops.

Chapter One

Here's how to write 45-minute one-act plays for teenagers or older adult actors and audiences.

How to Write Plays & Skits from Life Stories or Current Events

Are you looking for the appropriate 45-minute, one-act play for high-school students or other teenagers, for community center drama worshops, or even for home school projects or for events and celebrations? Are you seeking one-act plays for older adults drama workshops? Use personal or biographical experiences as examples when you write your skit or play. If you want a really original play, write, revise, and adapt your own plays, skits, and monologues. Here's how to do it.

One-act plays usually run about 45 minutes and are about 45 pages in length. Allow a minute per page of playwriting. Begin by using specific examples taken from current events, history, or interview someone to record significant life events such as a role played in life or surviving an event. For skits and plays taken from significant life events or true stories, record your personal experience, personal history, or biographical resources.

Start with a general statement. Then relate the general to your specific personal experience. You don't have to only write about yourself. You can write about someone else as long as you have accurate historical facts about that person, and you state your credible resources that can be fact-checked for accuracy.

Here's an example of two opening sentences that state the general and then give the specific personal experience. "Mom's a space garbage woman. She repairs satellites."

Let's analyze all the different parts of an informed argument essay. By analyzing the result in depth instead of only skimming for breadth, you will be able to write concretely from different points of view.

You'll learn how to construct a full-length play from bare bones—from its concept. You start with a concept. Then you add at least three specific examples to your concept until it develops into a mold. A mold is a form, skeleton or foundation. Think of concept as conception. Think of mold as form or skeleton. Think of awning as the outer skin that covers the whole essay and animates it into lively writing.

You don't want your play to be spoken in a monotone. You want writing that is animated, alive, with active voice, and able to move, motivate, or inspire readers. Finally, you cover the mold with an awning. Look for tone, texture, and mood in your words, especially in the verbs and nouns.

The mold is your pit, skeleton or foundation. Your mold contains your insight, foresight, and hindsight. It has the pitfalls to avoid and the highlights. You need to put flesh on its bones.

Then you need to cover your mold with an awning. You need to include or protect that concept and mold or form by including it under this awning of a larger topic or category. The awning holds everything together. It's your category under which all your related topics fall. That's what the technique of organizing your essay or personal history is all about.

In abstract words, concept equals form plus details. In concrete words, story equals attitude plus details. That's the math formula for writing a play or skit if you'd like to put it into a logical equation of critical thinking. $C = Fo + De$. That's what you need to remember about writing a play based on life stories or history: your concept is composed of your form (mold, foundation, or skeleton) and details. A concept isn't an idea. It's the application of your idea. The application of your idea is revealed with the attitude of each character plus the events that happen to them based on their choices. It's like life.

A concept is what your story is about. Your concept is imbedded in your story. A story can mean your personal history or any other story or anecdote in your essay, or any highlight of your life or specific life experience. A concept also can be a turning point such as rites of passage or take place at any stage of life.

Before you write a monologue, skit, or play, write it first as a short slice of life vignette. This means take a slice of life and show what happens when a significant event impacts that character's slice of life or life story highlight. A vignette is short, usually about 1,000-1,500 words. Vignettes usually are read in five to seven minutes.

Then you can go back and add the drama as events unfold. When writing the informed argument, you will be able to give examples backed up with resources. That's what makes an essay great—knowing what examples to put into the essay at which specific points in time.

Gone will be general, vague, or sweeping statements. Analyze and discuss the parts that chronologically will be included in your skit, play, or monologue. Take each act of the enclosed play apart as you would take a clock or computer apart. Then put it back together with one act instead of three. Either condense the three acts into one short act about 45 pages in length lasting 45 minutes, or use one of the acts as the entire play. You would have to add some drama to bring one of the acts up to be read or acted in 45 minutes.

Now all the parts fit and work. Taking apart a play or monologue helps you understand how to plan and write your own essay-writing assignments or personal history as a time capsule. You also can re-write the monologue to become a 45-minute, 45-page one-act play. Experiment with the monologue and with the three-act play to see what parts you might want to take out or keep as you develop your one-act play.

How do you interpret family history as creative writing, and how do you interpret ancestry-related DNA tests? Everyone's life is worth a play, skit, monologue, or novel. Adapt any type of life story or historical event to a one-act play. To start, begin with a slice of life, a significant event or turning point that you will dramatize and turn into a one-act play suitable for a high-school drama workshop.

           *   *   *

Here Are 50 Strategies on How to Write A Life Story as a Play, Skit, or Monologue.

1. Contact anyone's family members to gain permission to write their family member's memorials.
2. Write memoirs of various clerical or other religious or social leaders.
3. Write two to four dozen memorials for houses of worship. Put these memorials in a larger book of memoirs for various organizations, religious groups, houses of worship, or professional associations.
4. Find a model for your biographies.

5. These could be based on a book of vocational biographies or centered on any other aspect of life such as religious or community service as well as vocations.

6. Read the various awards biographies written and presented for well-known people.

7. Focus on the accomplishments that stand out of these people or of you if you're writing an autobiography.

8. Use oral eulogies as your foundation. You'll find many oral eulogies that were used in memorial services.

9. Consult professionals who conduct memorial services to look at their eulogies written for a variety of people and presented at memorial services.

10. Stick to the length of a eulogy. You'll find the average eulogy runs about 1,500 to 1,800 words. That' is what's known as magazine article average length. Most magazines ask for feature articles of about 1,500 words. So your eulogies should run that same length.

11. When read aloud, they make up the eulogy part of a memorial service. At 250 to 300 words double-spaced per page, it comes to about five-to-seven pages and is read aloud in about seven to 10 minutes.

12. Take each 1,500-1,800 word eulogy and focus on the highlights, significant events, and turning points. Cut the eulogy down to one page of printed magazine-style format.

13. Keep the eulogy typeset so that it all fits on one page of printed material in 12 point font.

14. You can package one-page eulogies for memorial services or include a small photo on the page if space permits.

15. Cut the eulogy down to 50-70 words, average 60 words for an oral presentation using PowerPoint software for a computer-based slide show complete with photos.

16. Put the PowerPoint show on a CD or DVD. Use the shorter eulogy focusing on significant points in the person's life. The purpose of a PowerPoint eulogy is to show the person lived a purposeful life—a design-driven, goal-driven life with purpose and concrete meaning in relation to others.

17. Write biographies, memoirs, and autobiographies by focusing on the highlights of someone's life or your own life story. Turn personal histories into life stories that you can launch in the media. You need to make a life story salable. It is already valuable.

18. Read autobiographies in print. Compare the autobiographies written by ghostwriters to those written by the authors of autobiographies who write about their own experiences.

19. Read biographies and compare them to autobiographies written by ghost writers and those written as diary novels in first person or as genre novels in first person. Biographies are written in third person.

20. If you write a biography in third person keep objective. If you write an autobiography in first person you can be subjective or objective if you bring in other characters and present all sides of the story equally.

21. If you're writing a biography, whose memories are you using? If you write an autobiography, you can rely on your own memory. Writing in the third person means research verifying facts and fact-checking your resources for credibility. How reliable is the information?

22. Use oral history transcriptions, personal history, videos, audio tapes, and interviews for a biography. You can use the same for an autobiography by checking for all sides of the story with people involved in the life story—either biography or autobiography.

23. With personal histories and oral histories, be sure to obtain letters of permission and to note what is authorized. Celebrities in the public eye are written about with unauthorized or authorized biographies. However, people in private life who are not celebrities may not want their name or photo in anyone's book. Make sure everything you have is in writing in regard to permissions and what information is permitted to be put into your book or article, especially working with people who are not celebrities and those who are.

24. When interviewing, get written approval of what was said on tape. Let the person see the questions beforehand to be able to have time to recall an answer with accuracy regarding facts and dates or times of various events. Give peoples' memories a chance to recall memories before the interview.

25. Write autobiographies in the first person in genre or diary format. You can also dramatize the autobiography in a play or skit first and then flesh it out into novel format. Another alternative is to focus only on the highlights, events, and turning points in various stages of life.

26. Ghost-written autobiographies usually are written in the first person. A ghost-writer may have a byline such as "*as told to*" or "*with*____(name of ghostwriter)."

27. Condense experience in small chunks or paragraphs. Use the time-capsule approach. Use vignettes. Focus on how people solved problems or obtained

results or reached a goal. Find out whether the person wants you to mention a life purpose. Emphasize how the person overcame challenges or obstacles.

28. In an autobiography, instead of dumping your pain on others because it may be therapeutic for you, try to be objective and focus on what you learned from your choices and decisions and how what you learned transformed your life. Be inspirational and nurturing to the reader. Tell how you learned, what you learned, how you rose above your problems, and how you transcended the trouble. Focus on commitment and your relationship to others and what your purpose is in writing the autobiography.

29. Stay objective. Focus on turning points, highlights, and significant events and their relationship to how you learned from your mistakes or choices and rose above the trouble. Decide what your life purpose is and what points you want to emphasize. If you want to hide facts, decide why and what good it will do the reader. Stay away from angry writing and focus instead on depth and analysis.

30. Don't use humor if it puts someone down, including you. Don't put someone down to pick yourself up.

31. Make sure your writing doesn't sound like self-worship or ego soothing. Don't be modest, but don't shock readers either.

32. Before you write your salable autobiography, find out where the market is and who will buy it. If there is no market, use print-on-demand publishing and select a title most likely to be commercial or help market your book. At least you can give copies to friends and family members. Or self-publish with a printer. Another way to go is to self-publish using print-on-demand software yourself. Then distribute via advertising or the Internet and your Web site.

33. You'd be surprised at how many people would be interested in your life story if it were packaged, designed, and promoted. So launch your life story in the media before you publish. Write your life story as a novel or play or both. Every life story has value. I believe all life stories are salable. The hard part is finding the correct niche market for your experiences. So focus on what you are and what you did so people with similar interests, hobbies, or occupations may learn from you. Market to people who are in the same situation as you are.

34. Divide your biography into the 12 stages of life. Then pare down those 12 significant events or turning points and rites of passage into four quarters—age birth to 25 (young adult), age 26-50 (mature adult), age 51-75 (creative adult) and age 76-100 (golden years of self fulfillment).

35. Start with a vignette focusing on each of the most important events and turning points of your life. Do the same in a biography, only writing in third person. For your own life story, write in first person.

36. What's important for the reader to know about your life in relation to social history and the dates in time? For example, what did you do during the various wars?

37. Keep a journal or diary, and record events as they happen. Focus on how you relate to social history. Write in your diary each day. Use the Web and create a diary or Web *blog*.

38. If you keep a daily journal, and make sure it is saved on a computer disk or similar electronic diary, you can put the whole journal together and create a book or play online or have a digital recording of your life. It's your time capsule in virtual reality.

39. A daily journal will keep memories fresh in your mind when you cut down to significant events for a book. You want to recall significant events in detail with resources.

40. If you're young, keep a daily journal on a computer disk and keep transferring it from one technology to the next as technology evolves. Keep a spare saved and up on the Web so you can download it anytime. Use some of the free Web site space available to people online.

41. If you write a book when you're older, at least you'll have all the youthful memories in detail where you can transfer the notes from one computer to another or upload from your disk to a browser for publication with a print-on-demand publisher.

42. Keep writing short vignettes. Include all the details as soon as possible after the event occurs. When you are ready to write a book, you'll be able to look back rationally and from a much more objective and mature perspective on the details. Then you can decide what to put into a salable life story that's about to be published.

43. Don't listen to people who tell you that if you are not famous, your life story is only fit for your own family because no one else will buy it. Fiddle-de-sticks!

44. There are events that happened to you or experiences in your line of work, travel, parenting, research, or lifestyle that people want to read because you have experiences to share.

45. Find a niche market of people with similar interests and market your life story to them.

46. Try out the waters first with a short vignette in magazines. If the magazines buy your vignette, your slice of life story, then you can write a book. Can you imagine if all the travelers and archaeologists, parenting experts and teachers didn't value their life story to the point that they thought it was fit only for relatives (who may be the only ones not interested in reading it because they already know your life story). In fact, your relatives may be angry at you for spilling the details to the public.

47. Instead, focus on that part of your life where you made a choice or decision with which everyone can identify. Inspire and motivate readers. If your experience is universal, we can all identify with it. We all go through the same stages of life.

48. So let us know how you overcame your obstacles, solved problems, and rose above the keen competition.

49. Or if you didn't, let us know how you learned to live with and enjoy your life. Readers want nourishment. If your life isn't about making a difference in the world, then write about how you handled what we all go through.

50. We want to read about the joy of life, and your design-driven life full of purpose, meaning, and inspiration. We want to read about the universal in you with which we can identify. Most of all readers want information in a life story or personal history from which we can make our own choices. Keep your life story as a novel to 12 to 24 short chapters. Write in short, readable chunks.

Chapter Two

Turning a Three-Act Play into a One-Act Play, Skit, or Monologue for High-School Age Actors and Dramatists

Turn the following three-act play into a one-act play by either condensing the entire play into only the significant highlights, using one of the acts and expanding when needed, or turning the monologue based on the play into a one-act play. Your result should be a one-act play that runs approximately 45 minutes (or is about 45 pages in length).

The play, skit, or monologue should be suitable for any high-school age class of actors. Use your creativity. You also can work with the monologue and the play or use the monologue instead of the three-act play to develop a one-act play. Keep the words suitable for teenage drama workshops. Remember that less pages of dialogue are better when writing or acting in high-school type plays or skits. Read the play aloud to check whether what you've written fits into a 45-minute slot for a one-act play. Keep the characters as few as possible, usually about 5 characters.

       *   *   *

The Play "Coney Island" and Monologue Included for Performances.

       *   *   *

Chapter One: The Play and Monologue for Performances

Coney Island

List of Characters in this Play:

Meir Cohen Levi, Father of Hadara and Husband of Tsipke

Hadara Cohen Levi, Baby in first chapter, then 9-year old girl, first person as narrator.

Benjamin, son of Meir

Tsipke, the mother of Hadara

The Arab Sheik as Hadara's first husband,

*Ahmed (not his real name)

Eric* (not his real name), Hadara's second husband

Mrs. Hesk, an older neighbor with a Yiddish accent

Hadara's two children as five-year olds:

Fawzi,

Samira

Hadara's two children as young adults: (17-20 age group)

Fawzi,

Samira

Sales clerk

In-laws:

Samintov

Mazeltov

Darlene, college friend of Hadara

Black Man, in Subway

Goldie, Darlene's mother

Classmates, 8th and 9th grade, ages 13 and 14

Neighbors

Paramedic

Friends

          *   *   *

Act I

Ext. Brooklyn, N.Y., Rainy Day, November 1941

AS CURTAIN RISES, WE SEE THE FRONT OF THE CONEY ISLAND APARTMENT BUILDING WHERE MEIR in front of his brick, four-family apartment house tries to adjust the lens on his box camera. He reacts to the invisible wind that slashes his face, covering his white hair and beard with his hands as his breath quickens in anger.

Whippet-wiry MEIR (age 47), a janitor, is dressed in patched janitor's coveralls. From inside the house echoes of Bach peal through the apartment and can be heard outside. OFFSTAGE WHERE HEAR THE SOUND EFFECTS OF A SUBWAY elevator line grinding by, drowning out the phonograph music.

TSIPKE (38), his wife, carries in one arm her blanketed two-week old daughter, HADARA. In her other arm, she tries to balance a bouquet of American Beauty roses.

The blanket keeps blowing over the baby's face as TSIPKE fidgets to straighten the blanket. The baby's nerve-shattering cry pierces the wind.

TSIPKE
Hurry and take the picture.
The baby's turning blue from the cold weather.

TSIPKE shouts at MEIR. And the shouts seem to be coming from a horde of women, SCREAMING together in fury.

We see the open mouth of TSIPKE. Her voice becomes an indistinguishable roar of needy demand as loud as the wind.

MEIR tries to focus the camera once more. TSIPKE smiles and tries to pose as he fidgets with the lens.

TSIPKE yells again and again, like a compelling tattoo.

TSIPKE
The baby's freezing, you jerk.

MEIR
Shut up! Damn it.
I'm trying to keep the lens from getting dusty.

TSIPKE
Hurry up, neurotic. She can't breathe. What are you standing there for, got your thumb up your butt?

MEIR'S temper cracks, and he lets fly with a right hook to her left chest. The baby slides from the blanket into a puddle of rain on the sidewalk. MEIR can't stop punching his wife. The deep, red American Beauty roses scatter in the rain near the baby's head.

Darkened Stage

New Scene

Lights Come on. Spotlight on the Darkened Bedroom.
Int. Nov. 1950, Same Brooklyn Apartment
Night

HADARA lies awake next to her mother in the rutted double bed in which they both sleep. MEIR, in the next bedroom, sleeps in twin beds with his 22-year old son, BENJAMIN. It's three in the morning. Outside the window WE HEAR THE SOUND EFFECTS OF the grinding subway train as it passes on its way from Coney Island. There's the sound of squealing metal cars as the train turns on the elevator line track.

TSIPKE
Remember when we played suffering?
I'd rub your belly, and your doll would be delivered like a baby?

TSIPKE laughs and hacks her cigarette cough.

HADARA rolls over, pulling her mass of hair from her eyes.

HADARA
Mom, are you a worrywart?

TSIPKE
No. Do I look that nervous?

TSIPKE pops the muscle up in her biceps to show how strong her muscles are.

HADARA
I'm tired of hearing about your lack of romance. I'm sick of your hands all over me playing "having a baby." It's always either how your mom gave you away when you were two, or, where daddy is off to by himself.

TSIPKE
Your father gave me gonorrhea. Where do you think he got it, in France during World War One?

HADARA
I'm not interested any more in listening to your complaints about daddy or your life story and how you ate out of garbage cans as a kid, or how dad's job is mopping toilets in the Navy yard. You just talk, but you don't change anything.

TSIPKE
You're nine today. You have to know.

HADARA
No, I don't. The radiator dried out the air again. Now my nose and throat's raw.

MEIR tiptoes out of his bedroom and crawls into bed with his wife.

MEIR
Move over.
What's the kid doing up so late?

HADARA
What are you doing here?

MEIR ignores her and takes off his pajamas, climbing into bed to make love to his wife.

HADARA
Get out of here.

TSIPKE
Leave the kid, alone, MEIR.

MEIR
You kicking me out of bed?

MEIR hesitates for a moment. TSIPKE is silent.

HADARA
I want to go back to sleep.

MEIR
Shut up, you tramp.

HADARA
Don't call me a tramp on my birthday.

MEIR
(Outraged)
Better you should be crippled.
You should have been born a boy.

TSIPKE
She says she got a high IQ

MEIR
I'll smash you one, you piece of garbage.

MEIR hurries his pajamas back on and storms out of the bedroom looking for something to smash. He finds a hammer in the living room and begins to smash all the keys on HADARA's piano. TSIPKE gets up and follows him into the living room.

TSIPKE
Stop. I saved for months to buy that old piano. My daughter's a talented artist.
When MEIR finishes smashing the piano keys, he goes for HADARA's violin.
MEIR puts his foot through the violin. HADARA cries.

TSIPKE jumps out of bed.

TSIPKE
All the kid's birthday presents!

MEIR
I'll teach you.

MEIR, having smashed the violin, finally storms into the bathroom where HADARA's new puppy is sleeping in its basket and holds the puppy's belly against the hot radiator pipe in the bathroom until it stops whimpering.

The more HADARA CRIES, the more TSIPKE backs away from her. MEIR comes out of the bathroom with his hammer in hand and begins to chase HADARA around the living room and into the kitchen, waving the hammer over his head.

MEIR
If I catch you, I'll cripple you.
Heads will roll before you'll become a tramp and shame me.

HADARA (**sobbing**)
I'm sorry. I'm sorry, daddy.

MEIR
Better you should be a cripple then to be born a girl and make trouble.

TSIPKE follows MEIR into the kitchen and lights a cigarette, making the motions of heating up water for coffee.

TSIPKE
Leave the kid alone.

MEIR (Raging)
I should have flushed her out into the bay with the condom before she was conceived. Better such a dog wasn't born.

TSIPKE
If I have to get up for a second cigarette...
Damn, those cigarettes are choking me.
But you two fighting all the time are driving me to smoke.

MEIR takes a swing at HADARA, but misses. HADARA darts out the kitchen and dashes through the living room and out the front door, running down the apartment steps to the basement. She hurries down the cellar steps with MEIR, chasing behind, hammer swinging over his head.

In the darkness of the cellar, MEIR chases HADARA. She squeezes her body into a partially-filled co&1 bin, hiding behind an old barrel. HADARA covers herself with coal.

MEIR peers around for a moment, wild-eyed. He wipes the sweat from his upper lip on his pajama sleeve.

MEIR
If I catch you, you die.

HADARA watches him from between the wide slats of the coal bin as he swings his hammer overhead. MEIR passes a basement worktable and puts down his hammer only to pick up an ax. He slaps the ax broadside across his thigh several times. Then he sighs and puts the ax back on the table. Finally, exhausted, MEIR plods up the wooden stairs. The apartment door closes with a bang.

Int. Kitchen Brooklyn Apartment. Same Night

TSIPKE
(staccato voice)
No sooner did I put the baby on your lap then you told me to take her off because she gave you an erection. Your temper is only a bad habit. Why is it necessary to transfer your stress to me? Why isn't it important that you add to my life span?

MEIR
You keep hounding me just because your step father came into your room to have sex with you when you went upstate to visit your mother.

TSIPKE
He's your richest brother. Besides, I told him to get out. You didn't see him grabbing an ax or hammer.

MEIR
Girls only make trouble. You know how many times I asked the doctor to check to make sure-maybe he made a mistake-maybe she was a boy.

TSIPKE
Is that why you never held a conversation with your own daughter? You never smiled.
Not once in your whole life did she ever hear you laugh, except at her.

MEIR
What about you going into your son's room to massage his feet every morning and comb his hair?

TSIPKE
I'm a Jewish mother.

MEIR
He's twenty-two. You're overbearing.

TSIPKE
And you're a cold fish. The only passion I ever see is anger.
If that's the only way you can get power, I'm going back to bed.

She turns around.

TSIPKE
Where's the kid?

MEIR
In the coal bins again.
Let her rot in hell down there.

MEIR staggers back to bed. TSIPKE sits on her bed with the light on, smoking cigarettes and reading old newspapers.

Darken Stage or Curtain.

New Scene:

Int. Basement Morning

HADARA peaks out of the basement window and scratches off some of the frost. She watches MEIR go off to work, walking toward the subway station. Then she climbs the stairs back to the apartment and knocks on the door.

TSIPKE opens the door wearing a stained and disheveled robe.

TSIPKE
Benjamin just had a fight with me over you making too much noise. And he broke a lamp over my arm. I dared him to do it.

HADARA
Does daddy know?

TSIPKE
I had to tell him.
So now he smashed your brother's typewriter right before his term paper is due.

HADARA
I'm too tired to go to school today.

HADARA slowly walks through the foyer, passing and looking at her dead canary in its small bird cage.

TSIPKE
It caught a cough.
You'll have to take it down to the garbage cans.

HADARA
Aw, no!

HADARA runs into the bedroom. TSIPKE follows her.

TSIPKE
Listen, you little mouse, want to go shopping?

HADARA
Don't you have anything better to do?

TSIPKE goes back into the kitchen and begins to fry eggs. HADARA comes into the kitchen. TSIPKE puts down a heel of rye bread for HADARA and some hot cocoa and corn flakes.

Darkened Stage, Curtain

New Scene:

In a department store near a counter with women's costume jewelry, lingerie, and cheap cologne…

Int. Department Store, Brooklyn Day

TSIPKE and HADARA walk through the department store. TSIPKE shoplifts baubles and silken wisps of lingerie, cheap cologne, and boxes of face powder,

rhinestone costume jewelry and lipsticks. When no one is in the ladies room, she taker in clothing and stuffs the items into her panties.

HADARA sneers.

TSIPKE
So that's why I wear incontinence panties. Bet you can't pronounce it.

HADARA
I don't want any of the beads or perfume. You've cursed them.
You've given them the evil eye. We'll get bad luck.
Why do you take things in tiny sizes, when you're shaped like an apple?

TSIPKE enters the toilet cubicle.

TSIPKE
(banging on the wall)
Your father gives me three dollars a day.
How else can I live like a lady instead of a woman?
HADARA
I won't wear that crap.

TSIPKE (handing her clothes under the stall)
Here, stuff this into your panties.

HADARA
No! How come women of grandma's generation never went to school in the old country?
And how come you dropped out in the fifth grade?

TSIPKE
I was born at the turn of the century.

HADARA
So were a lot of famous women scientists.

TSIPKE drags whining HADARA into the fitting room with some of the dresses and items tucked inside of three dresses because the sign says only three garments are allowed in the dressing room at one time.

In front of the mirror, TSIPKE tries on bras, slips, and clothing under her own clothes. But all she brings out are the three dresses she took in with her and hands them to the clerk. The rest are stashed on her person.

TSIPKE (to sales clerk)
These dresses aren't the right size.

TSIPKE leads HADARA by the hand into the shoe department to pick out a pair of school shoes for her. They sit down to rest in the shoe department. A salesman approaches. HADARA points to a pair of saddle shoes and the salesman retrieves the shoes. The SALESMAN tries to lace the saddle shoe on HADARA'S foot.

SHOE SALESMAN
Well, little girl. Give me that skinny foot, here.

HADARA
Leave me alone, you!

HADARA whispers in his ear and runs out of the shoe department.

SHOE SALESMAN

That filthy-mouthed kid.
I wonder where she learned that?

Embarrassed, TSIPKE gets up and leaves to chase after HADARA. She catches up with her and slaps her so hard she gets a bloody nose. TSIPKE buys a towel and makes HADARA keep it on her nose.

TSIPKE
Don't make me hit you.
Because if I do, I'll kill you.

HADARA
He didn't have to call me skinny.

TSIPKE
Horseface! Why did you say that word to him in this place?

HADARA
He meant I was ugly.

TSIPKE (Staring at HADARA'S feet)
You wore those old, dirty socks?

HADARA
It's from the coal bin.

TSIPKE
You're beginning to stink just like your old man who's never taken a bath since World War One.

Darkened Stage or Curtain End of Scene.

New Scene:
Back At Home.
Afternoon.

HADARA is reading two comic books, "The Vault of Horror" and "The Crypt of Terror. Mother and daughter are riding home, seated on the subway.

HADARA
See my scar? I don't know where you
Stop and I begin anymore.

TSIPKE
So?

HADARA
Your curse and evil eye made me fall over that fence last summer.
The year before, I got a fish hook in my leg.

TSIPKE
So it was my curse, was it? Does that explain the eight stitches they had to take in your chin? Now that you're a scar face, only the worse kind of man will want to marry you.

HADARA
That stuff you took. It brings me bad luck.

TSIPKE
Then don't touch it.

HADARA
I want to enroll myself in Hebrew School on Monday. Nobody talks to me in class in public school. I don't have any friends. And when I told the teacher, she gave me an "F" in personal relationships.

Fadeout to a Darkened Stage
Curtain Descends: End Of Scene.

New Scene

Tsipke's Apartment—1955—Day

HADARA
I'm damn tired of your analyzing me.

TSIPKE
Maybe I should go back to buying corporate high-yield bonds?

HADARA
(turns TSIPKE to mirror)
Go ahead, look at yourself stuffing negligees into old ladies incontinence panties.

TSIPKE
You think I wanted you?

HADARA
You hate kids, don't you?

TSIPKE
No. Damn you. I'm desperately lonely.
Are you worth the three dollars a day your old man flings at me?

HADARA
Are you?
You've never gone back to school after the fifth grade….never had a job, you lazy blimp.

TSIPKE
Why did you have to be born just as I was about to divorce your father?

HADARA
I hate weak mothers.

TSIPKE
A lady has a husband rich enough to support her. A woman has to work because she can't get a good enough man.

HADARA
Only failures marry.

TSIPKE
Think I wanted you?
I'm only taking care of you because your father made it my responsibility.

HADARA
What do you get from stealing…some kind of sexual excitement?

TSIPKE
What do you mean, sex?
I haven't had any since you were born.

HADARA
Do I have to know that?

TSIPKE
Horse face! Your father hasn't had a bath since the end of World War One.

HADARA
Is that why you're always saying he's a disabled veteran?

TSIPKE pauses a beat, looking disgusted. Then she slaps HADARA across the face. She retracts in horror.

HADARA
How the hell was I ever conceived?

TSIPKE
My father paid us a visit.

HADARA
What has that got to do with it?

TSIPKE
I was so happy to see him,
I gave him my room and went to sleep in your father's room.

HADARA
Did Benjamin watch the bang?

TSIPKE
(looking down)
He was sleeping, I guess.

HADARA
I wished daddy was proud of me.

TSIPKE
A caring man prefers olive oil instead of butter.

HADARA
See this scar on my face?

TSIPKE
What about the lightning you carved on my face?

HADARA
You called me horse face.

TSIPKE
But you are as ugly as your father.

HADARA
I don't look ugly.
I look Semitic.

TSIPKE
Better get yourself an exciting career because no man worth money will want you.

HADARA
I got that scar because you cursed me.
(shaking her mother)
Take it off. Take off the evil eye, damn it!

TSIPKE
You had no right to throw a protractor in my face.

HADARA
Your evil eye made me fall over that fence in the schoolyard and split my face open.

TSIPKE
You lost your balance because you were playing with A Syrian girl. She's a jynx to you because of some previous life.

HADARA
We were nine years old.

TSIPKE
I told you time and time again that people who are not the same as us are bad luck when we try to be them. When we can't see the boundaries, we don't know where we end and where they begin.

HADARA
No, it was your evil-eyed curse.

TSIPKE
She was with you when it happened. I wasn't anywhere near there.

HADARA
You linked minds with me when I threw the protractor at you. Or was it a compass?

TSIPKE
I didn't throw my mother's evil eye. It was karma.

HADARA
You're all crazy makers. All those churches you go to, those clubs, the gypsies you visit in storefronts to gab.

TSIPKE
I'm lonely. You did something bad to Syrians in a past life. That's why they're bad luck to you now.

HADARA
The girl simply asked me to pretend the janitor was chasing us.

TSIPKE
The little bitch didn't take your side, did she?
She forced you to climb the fence.

HADARA
I'd do anything for her friendship.

TSIPKE
It was her fantasy, not yours.
Can't you see? It was her karma cursing you.

HADARA
Stop, already.
We shouldn't even bring back her name.
She's a jinx.
Your father's mother's eye, those people from Bialystock, the musicians who played with the Klezmorim, they will put the curse of the evil on anyone who commits evil.

TSIPKE
How should I know?
Of course she's a jinx.
Maybe she put a curse on all of us.
Isn't it odd that her brother-in-law turned out to be the lawyer for the city and we lost the case?

HADARA
We make our own choices.

TSIPKE
I had to pay all the lawyer's costs.

HADARA
I've got to change my name.

TSIPKE
Why do you let strangers torture you?
Isn't it enough you have this family?

HADARA
Why did you tell me the Japanese were bombing New York when I was three?

TSIPKE
Such trouble, such complications from you, horse face.

HADARA
That's my first memory.
You enjoyed making me sweat and tremble.

TSIPKE
I could feel your father moving inside my body.

HADARA
But it was me in your arms.

TSIPKE
Now your mind has the strength of ten men.

HADARA
Dad keeps saying he wished he'd flushed me into the bay.

TSIPKE
I'd be free, if only I sent your brother to the drug store for rubbers.

HADARA
Free to do what—make lopsided ash trays in your ceramics class?

TSIPKE
You think your soul can be flushed through your dad's kidneys?

HADARA
If you knew how much I hate being female.

TSIPKE
The day I married, I wrote in my diary "Today I died."

HADARA
Then stop saying I'm killing you.

TSIPKE
Your old man read it back to me with tears in his eyes.
We were on the honeymoon train to Miami.

HADARA
He opened your secret diary?

TSIPKE
Girls make trouble.

HADARA
Emotions make trouble.
My only need is to get rid of them.

TSIPKE
Through the storms of hell, I curse you to be logical.
You'll get your wish…in your husband.

HADARA
Why are you afraid to be Jewish? Polish Jewish, I mean?

TSIPKE
Shut up.
They'll getcha.

HADARA
You're a holocaust survivor, aren't you, mom. Aren't you?
Why don't you ever talk about it?

TSIPKE
The second generation mustn't know.

HADARA
Would it really have made a difference?

TSIPKE
They said I had the map of Jerusalem printed on my face.

HADARA
You were beaten by strangers who didn't even know your name.

TSIPKE
They were biting my tits off.
And I was screaming that my hair is black because I'm from Babylon.

HADARA
What did you do with the fear, pass it onto me?

TSIPKE
I bleached my hair, and changed my name.

HADARA
People change with time.

TSIPKE
You think it's a joke?

HADARA
I'll tell you where the holocaust is, mom.
It's inside this dump.

TSIPKE
Don't belittle the holocaust.
I take your father's and brother's slaps like a soldier.

HADARA
And all you do is nag and laugh at him…and complain. But nothing changes.
I'm growing up to fear all men.
He says you're overbearing.

TSIPKE
Your brother is my life.
You're father is always at his flower shows.
And I'm all alone, except for you.
So would you lighten up?

HADARA
I'll laugh at my own pain if I want to, walrus-face, manatee-hips…guilt complex.

TSIPKE
You have a moustache.

HADARA
Thanks for reminding me.

TSIPKE
Hey, what the hell did you ever do for me?

Curtain or Fade Out

Act II

New Scene:

Jr. High School Classroom Fall 1955 Day

It is the fall of 1955 at a public junior high school in Brooklyn. HADARA (age 13) sits in a classroom that is made up of mostly Syrian Jewish students whose parents are recent immigrants from either Syria or Syria by way of Latin America.

It is break time in home room, when students are free to chat. JUSTA, (13) and Seeley (13) are Syrian Pampered princesses who sit in the surrounding seats near HADARA.

These girls are so wealthy they make uptown Jewish princesses look like paupers. They all live around Ocean Parkway, the wealthiest street in Flatbush, in private homes as big as mansions.

HADARA at 13 is a short, skinny girl with waist-length black hair in corkscrew curls and pale green eyes hidden behind coke-bottle thick eyeglasses.

HADARA
Why can't I join your sorority?
The Megaz looks like a lot of fun.

JUSTA
You have to be Syrian to join.

HADARA
Well what if I said I was a Syrian Jewish Princess who spent all day shopping and had a big house like you instead of a two-room apartment?

JUSTA
You ain't got any Syrian name or Syrian money.

HADARA
That means nothing.
What if I had a Syrian bio father and a Polish Jewish step father or somethin'?

JUSTA
I haven't seen you around any Syrian neighborhoods. You don't even live near our blocks. I've never seen you go to the Syrian synagogue.

HADARA
How do you know what synagogue I go to?
Besides, my mom is so scared of being Jewish, she drags me to churches.
She got beat up plenty just for looking like the stereotype.

JUSTA
Your family doesn't hang around with our crowd at the Nobeh parties we have on Saturday nights. You're not even religious. You wear lipstick. I've never seen you around before.

HADARA
Well, what if I hang around the Syrian center?
Suppose I insist I am Syrian and I want to join.
I have a special reason for wanting to join the Megaz.

I want to find a rich husband to cherish me.
What would I have to do to get in?

JUSTA
Pass initiation. You have to take off all your clothes in Seeley's closet and let her six-year old brother feel you up.

HADARA
I couldn't do such a thing.

JUSTA
Did you ever let a boy feel you up?

Justa giggles and starts to chew on her snack.

HADARA
Is that your stupid initiation rites?

JUSTA
You have to take off your sweater and bra in Seeley's closet and walk into her living room and stand there while Tynie feels you up.

HADARA
What about Seeley's mother?

JUSTA
She's in Florida for a week.
The maid finishes the ironing at two and leaves to go shopping.
We're nearly fourteen.
We don't need the maid to watch us every minute.

HADARA
If I take off my clothes are you sure I can join the Megaz?

JUSTA
Do you want to join?

HADARA
You're pretty weird.

Int. Seeley's House

Seeley, Robrana, Wiley, and dusts, the leaders of the Megaz sorority of Syrian Jewish junior high girls meets at Seeley's house on Ocean Parkway in Brooklyn. All the girls are 13 and go to the same junior high school.

No parent is present in the large, mansion-like private home. The heavy, black maid is busy ironing clothes and walks out a few minutes after all the girls arrive and settle down, lady-like and quiet in the spacious, plush living room.

HADARA
I heard all of your parents come from one city in Syria—Aleppo.
Is it true the Aleppan Jews don't hang around with the Jews from Damascus?
Is it like the Litvaks and the Galicianas used to be fifty years ago in Europe?

HADARA looks around the house, pacing the floor nervously.

SEELEY
All I know is that we have two social centers.
One in Bensonhurst for the Damascenes.
And there's one here for the Haleebees from Aleppo.
Our grandparents were born in Aleppo
My mom is from South America.

Seeley looks at JUSTA wide-eyed. The two girls exchange glances and nudge one another's elbows, smiling and giggling.

JUSTA
We're all Syrians.

HADARA
Give me something proud to be a Litvak.
Of what can I be proud?
Of what I do instead of who I am?
Give me something proud to say about being a Litvak?

JUSTA
You can be proud you're in the same classroom at school with us and everyone else.

HADARA
Oh, so you do talk to me.
How come you don't marry
Ashkenazi Jews from Europe?
You think Sephardics or Mizrahi are better or older?
Equal, but different, like men and women?
You think we're self-styled Jews from Northern Europe?
Maybe you think we're part Vikings and Asians.

JUSTA
We never saw you around our social center.

HADARA
I stood outside the Syrian synagogue on the holidays.
So, I hear Davie Joseph is practicing for his Bar Mitzvah.
He's probably right next door.

JUSTA
Hadara, you know what you have to do.
It's initiation time.

HADARA
Sure. Whereas your closet?

It's dark in the hallway as HADARA enters Seeley's huge closet and takes off her sweater end undershirt.

She stays in there a long while, as the girls pass around plates of Syrian pizza—cheese and spices melted on top of Pita bread.

SEELEY
What are you doing in there so long?

HADARA
I'm ready.

After a long moment of torment, HADARA walks out in nude-colored body suit from the waist up, clutching her undershirt and sweeter to her undeveloped chest. Justa pulls her sweater and undershirt out of her grip as HADARA crosses her arms over her chest to hide her flat breasts.

Justa tosses her clothing high in the air to Seeley, then to Robrana and to Wiley. The clothes continuously are tossed in the air from girl to girl as if they were & volley ball.

ELLEY
Monkey in the middle.
The Polish girl plays a fiddle.

HADARA
Give me beck my clothes. Please, girls.

HADARA paces around chasing after the girls, trying to form same eye contest to get their attention and get her clothing back. She keeps her hands crossed over her chest.

HADARA
Where's your six-year old brother? You lied to me. He's not here.
He'd probably tell your parents.

ELLEY
Hey, Seeley. Give her back her clothes.
Go on give it to her.

JUSTA
Oh, gee. All right. Here's your sweater.

JUSTA tosses the sweater and HADARA reaches up to catch her clothing in mid-air. The girls giggle loudly.

SEELEY
Look how small her breasts are. She's as flat as a pancake.

HADARA's back is toward the camera. The girls stop in their tracks and all of them stare at HADARA's naked chest as she struggles to put her torn under-shirt on and then her red sweater.

JUSTA
We have no initiation rights to join the Megaz We just wanted to see how crazy you'd act to get into our sorority.

HADARA
You really went and did it.

JUSTA
Why did you lie and keep insisting you were Syrian? I know where you live, in a roachy apartment next to the subway and not in the Syrian neighborhood.

HADARA
I'll have to face you in school tomorrow and for the next three years.

SEELEY
Crazy HADARA is really nuts enough to get naked to join our club.

JUSTA
A Crazy HADARA.
You have to be born one of us to join.

JUSTA opens the door and shoves HADARA into the street. She backs up and the four girls pace toward until HADARA is standing at the curb. Then the girls toss her into the street into the path of an oncoming car. The car brakes and comes to a halt a few inches before hitting HADARA.

HADARA looks up only to see Avy Joseph, the Syrian Jewish boy' she has a crush on coming out of the Synagogue after practicing for his Bar Mitzvah. Their eyes meet, but each turns and quickly walks in two opposite directions, to offstage. Avy is dressed in a prayer shawl and skull cap. He had been practicing for his Bar Mitzvah.

The girls go back into the house, giggling and slam door shut. HADARA is left standing on the curb in silence as Avy Joseph approaches as he is on his way home nearby.

HADARA
Hello Avy. How's school?

AVY
Pretty good.

AVY walks away quickly, not paying any attention to HADARA.

Soon a swarm of teenage girls leave the synagogue end catch up to AVY as HADARA watches from a short distance away, unnoticed. The girls crowd around AVY as he stands with crossed legs, leaning on the fence of one of the areas upscale homes chatting with them. He's popular with the girls as they smile and admire the dimples in his cheeks.

Darken Stage: Curtain.

End of Scene

New Scene:

Eight Years Later In Time:

Fade In:

August, 1963

Int.—Dance Hall—YMCA—New York City—Night

An uncrowded dance-hall floor is livened by classical Flamenco guitar music. "El Judio" is playing—a Middle Eastern-sounding wild, Flamenco dance. HADARA swirls onto the dance floor, alone. She's wearing white, with long, fringy ear rings.

Her hands clap in the soft, seductive rhythms of southern Spain, the beat builds in a crescendo with the music. Then she begins to dance by herself.

The music grows louder, the dancing wilder as a crowd forms around her. HADARA is now twenty-one years of age.

She's a petite, slender woman with long black hair and dark, compelling eyes. Hadara finishes her dance. Someone puts on American dance records of the sixties. One man, MALEK, 28, a Lebanese exchange student walks toward HADARA.

MALEK
Thanks for editing my technical manual.

HADARA
No sweat.
I doubt if I could write a book in Arabic.

MALEK
Hey, introduce me to that blonde who walked in with you.

**MALEK points to HADARA's girlfriend, ANDREA.
She's a tall, buxom blonde.**

HADARA
Sure. Oh, Andrea!
Meet an old friend—
Malek Edeen. He's a good, Druish boy from Beirut.

MALEK
That's a Druze.
My religion is Druze, from Lebanon.

ANDREA
Hi! Has HADARA been writing your master's thesis?

MALEK
Technical manuals.
Would you like to dance?

ANDREA
No. I'm supposed to meet this violin-playing Afghan urologist.

MALEK
You look German.
Is that where you're from?

ANDREA
I'm a Polish Jew from West First Street, *near* Coney Island just as Cleopatra was
from Alexandria, *near* Egypt.

HADARA
Malek, Andrea only dates foreign Jewish doctors from Asia.

ANDREA
The ones born here want wives whose fathers are rich enough to set them up in business.

HADARA
She's joking.

MALEK
Say, I have a friend who came from Syria only five days ago.

HADARA
And you want me to teach him English.

MALEK
He doesn't speak a word.

HADARA
All I know in Arabic is "ya habeeby."

MALEK
I'll interpret.

HADARA and MALEK walk out of the dance hall to a quiet area of the YMCA with lounge chairs and desks.

HADARA
What does he do for a living?

MALEK
He's a year away from his doctorate in engineering.

HADARA
Hmm…a good provider.

MALEK
The guy speaks German.
He lived in Frankfort for the past six years.

HADARA
A doctor of engineering!
What kind?

MALEK
Mechanical.
Is that a good enough provider?

HADARA
That's not as good as matching me to a military colonel.
But it's easier than trying to marry a doctor in New York.

MALEK
Who said anything about marrying the guy?

HADARA
Oh, flesh out.

HADARA
What kind of a visa does he have?

MALEK
A thirty-day one.

HADARA
He's desperate.

MALEK
How come you stopped dating me?

HADARA
You're a mechanic.
I told you I'm looking to marry a professional.

MALEK
What would he see in you?

HADARA
Hey, we all go into marriage looking for a package deal.

MALEK
It's a trade-off.

HADARA
The most successful guys still have to settle.

MALEK
And what are you peddling?

HADARA
I'm a college graduate…worked my way through.
What's the least stressful job? That's what I want.

MALEK
That won't make you rich.

HADARA
Don't I deserve a prince?

MALEK and HADARA meet up with AHMED HADDAD.
They shake hands.

MALEK
Well, here's your sheik.

MALEK speaks in Arabic to AHMED, who nods, smiling.
The conversation is conducted entirely through MALEK, the interpreter.

HADARA
Are you sure you're an engineer?

MALEK
(in Arabic the translated in English by Malek)
Tell her what you do.

AHMED
(in Arabic, then translated in English by Malek)
I'm a mechanical engineer babysitting for an Arab family on Long Island in
exchange for a room.

MALEK
Tell her about you getting a doctorate in engineering.

AHMED
(in Arabic then translated by Malek in English)
I've got a year to go.

MALEK
What do you say we all go to chat in an all-night automat?

AHMED
Let's shove off.

They head for the subway.

End of Scene: Curtain.

EXT. SUBWAY ENTRANCE

INT. SUBWAY

INT. AUTOMAT—NEW YORK—NIGHT

MALEK
Ahmed says he's on a thirty-day visa and has to find a wife, fast.

HADARA
Good luck.

AHMED
(in Arabic)
I want lots of children.

MALEK
He's ready to start a family.

HADARA
Children only make a woman poor.

MALEK
He has no money.

HADARA
I don't want to be dragged to the level of my husband's job.

MALEK
Careful, Ahmed's an aimed bullet.

HADARA
How ironic New York Jews aren't invited to work in Lebanon.

MALEK
What brought that out?

HADARA
Imagine being arrested for looking convexed-nosed in a Phoenician world where everybody else looks convexed rather than perplexed.

MALEK
(looking at his watch)
Yallah! Look at the time.
The last bus leaves for Hoboken at three A.M.
I'll walk you to the Times Square subway entrance.

They all rise and leave the eatery, walking to the Forty-Second Street subway entrance. AHMED drapes his arm around HADARA and she looks into his smiling eyes.

AHMED
(in German)
Do you speak any German?

HADARA
I only speak English.
Say…"I speak some English."

AHMED
I speak some English.

HADARA
There. I'll have you talking with a Brooklyn accent in three months.

A clock in a store window reads 2:30 A.M. They look up at the clock.
They reach the subway entrance. MALEK pays HADARA's subway fare, putting a token in the turnstile.

MALEK
Thanks for the English lesson.

MALEK pauses, looking down, then at his watch. He turns and walks away.
AHMED follows behind.

HADARA
What? Aren't you two gentleman going to take this lady home?

MALEK
(shouting back)
I'm talking Ahmed home.
There's no way I'm missing the last bus.

MALEK storms off, shoving AHMED to hurry.
HADARA kicks the wall in the subway station.

HADARA
(shouting to Malek)
It's an hour's ride back to Coney Island.

End of Scene.
New Scene: Inside of Subway Car.

HADARA is wearing a fancy white dress and spike heels.
She takes the D-train to her Brooklyn station, KINGS HIGHWAY.

Opposite her sits a middle-aged black man with a frightening, badly-scarred
face. He's dressed in filthy, torn clothes and wears a cap.

He smiles sardonically and stares at her during the entire subway trip.
HADARA closes her eyes and pretends to sleep for most of the trip.

When the train stops at KINGS HIGHWAY, the black man follows her, ducking behind the KINGS HIGHWAY station sign when she turns around to see whether anyone's following her.

He hides. She isn't aware he's following her until she starts to walk the short distance to her four-family apartment house.

The black man catches up to her by an open lot, just a few feet from her house. He puts his hand on her shoulder and she spins around to look into his frightening face.

BLACK MAN
Hi! baby.

HADARA gives him a look of terror. She bolts and makes a run for it. We see her spike heels trying to run. Her tight skirt hobbles her, and he catches up, grabbing her and throwing her to the ground.

HADARA
My purse. Take it.
There's only a dollar.

BLACK MAN
Shut up.

HADARA thrusts her cloth shoulder bag in his face. He grabs it and tosses it in the lot. He drags her in the high weeds and begins to strangle her.

HADARA closes her eyelids a splinter and pretends she's unconscious. He releases his thumbs from around her throat as she makes herself limp.

BLACK MAN drags HADARA over the curb, hidden behind a parked car. He lifts her skirt and shoves his hand into her panties. He bends over and looks closely at her face to catch a reaction. HADARA opens her eyes and gives him a fierce look of disgust.

BLACK MAN
Bitch. Don't say a word.
Think you can fool me?
Tryin' to pass for white?

Bitch. Shut up.
Tryin' to pass for white. Yes.

BLACK MAN spits on the ground next to her. HADARA screams. He puts his hand over her mouth. She quiets. He tears off her glasses and stomps them until they shatter. He loses his cap. He drags HADARA further under the curb, against the tires of the parked car.

BLACK MAN begins to strangle HADARA more violently. She closes her eyes. Instantly a window in the apartment house across the street opens quickly with a very loud creak. BLACK man is startled as he looks up. In the window is a very old lady.

MRS. HESK
(in a thick, Yiddish accent)
You pishikas, get the hell off my stoop.
Why you Hassids foolin' around so late?
It's Shabbos. It's Tish B'Av.

BLACK man is startled and runs away.

HADARA rubs her neck and staggers to her feet.

HADARA
Mrs. Hesk, Please, Mrs. Hesk, Call the police.
I've just been strangled and almost raped.

MRS. HESK
Are you all right?
I wish you pishikas wouldn't make so much noise.

HADARA
I said strangled! Would you call the police, already?

MRS. HESK
I'm calling. I'm calling for you.

HADARA sits down on her stoop and waits for the police car to arrive. She rests her head in her hands and sobs. The police car arrives with two officers.

FIRST OFFICER
So you're the girl whose boyfriend got fresh and to get revenge, you're sending us on a wild goose chase?

HADARA
No. Why don't you believe me?
I was strangled and almost raped by this black guy who followed me from the subway to my house.

SECOND OFFICER
Were you raped?

HADARA
No. I was almost murdered!
The jerk shoved two fingers into my vagina.
Am I still a virgin?
Could I catch V.D.?

FIRST OFFICER

Look, if your boyfriend got fresh…

HADARA
If I had a boyfriend to protect me, this wouldn't have happened.

FIRST OFFICER
Okay. I just want to make sure.

SECOND OFFICER
These are whore's hours. Why were you on the subway so late alone?

HADARA
(looks annoyed)
I went to a club meeting, met some people, and talked.
They walked me to the subway.
I can't see without my glasses.
He smashed them.

SECOND OFFICER searches the empty lot.

SECOND OFFICER
There's a cap. It looks like the kind they usually wear.

HADARA
Can't you see all the broken glass?

FIRST OFFICER
What do you do?

HADARA
I'm a creative writing major at NYU.
My minor is film and archaeology.
I want to be a visual anthropologist someday.

FIRST OFFICER
Age?

HADARA
Twenty-one.

SECOND OFFICER
Would you like a police ambulance?

HADARA
Of course.
Can't you see my neck?
And I have a sociology exam on Monday.

The police car leaves. HADARA sits on the stoop and waits for the ambulance, rubbing her bruised neck.

CUT TO:
Ambulance paramedic walks over.

PARAMEDIC
Are you the one?

HADARA
My horoscope saved me.
Hey, can I catch V.D?
That creep poked his cruddy nails into my vagina.

PARAMEDIC
Not unless he scratched you there.

HADARA
Now how am I supposed to know whether I'm scratched?
I was too busy worrying about getting strangled.

PARAMEDIC
Hop in. You'll be okay.

HADARA
No I won't.
You're going to send me a bill for fifty bucks for this ride.

PARAMEDIC
You should only live so long.

HADARA
(talking to paramedic)
The hospital smacks me for another hundred.
How come I'm attacked and I get to pay for my exam?

End of Scene. Curtain.

New Scene

CUT TO:

INT. DARLENE LEVINE'S HOUSE—SEPT. 1963—DAY

DARLENE LEVINE (25) is a judge's single daughter who lives in a plush private home in Jamaica Estates, a wealthy suburb of New York (Queens).

She is HADARA's best friend and confident at NYU. But DARLENE has dropped out of school to travel and husband-hunting, both without success.

HADARA arrives in the afternoon.
ANGLE ON GOLD DOOR KNOCKER and mahogany door. DARLENE opens the door, greeting HADARA with a smile.

HADARA walks into the house, lavishly covered and plush with paintings DARLENE and her mother have created.

DARLENE
What's the big emergency?

HADARA
Don't I have to confide in somebody?

The two young women take seats opposite each other on the plush white sofa.

DARLENE
I met the sexiest guy at Grossingers.

HADARA
But he's bald.

DARLENE
And paunchy at twenty-nine.

HADARA
You let a good provider go?

DARLENE
There's no way he could support me the way my father does.

HADARA
Is he available?

DARLENE
I'll never leave my parent's home.

HADARA
If I had a good job,
I'd leave today.

DARLENE
Would you trade all this for a roach-wracked studio in Greenwich Village?
I guess you're either born lucky or born rich.
Which are you?

HADARA grabs DARLENE by the shoulders and grins at her.

HADARA
You don't work.
I'm wearing myself out to finish college at night, slaving in a typing pool all day.
Yes, it's better than my granny's sweat shop job from the triangle building fire days.
What do you do? Live off your daddy's trust fund?
Or are you still living at home at age twenty-five?

DARLENE
Shop. Travel. Brunch.
Design and sew my own clothes and live at home waiting to inherit.

HADARA
You're an animal.

DARLENE
(**sipping tea, eating**)
You're weird, but then all creative writing majors are different than us secretarial science students.

HADARA
Guess what's news? My mom's just been arrested for shoplifting.
And my brother's the lawyer who's defending her.

DARLENE
I've got an appointment with my own therapist today.
Now I have something to tell her.

HADARA
I'm so ashamed of being ashamed.

DARLENE
How'd they nab her?

HADARA
With a sexy nightie draped over her arm.

DARLENE
Is she crazy?

HADARA
No, but she's not a fair-weather friend like I just realized you are.
Mom weighs two hundred fifty pounds.
But the nightie was a size six. I wear a size fourteen.

DARLENE retrieves some muffins from a plate and serves them with tea.

DARLENE
My mom just won a prize for her latest screenplay.

HADARA
And my mom walked out of the store in a daze from her high blood pressure pills.
The security guard tackled her to the ground, smashing her head against the
pavement.

DARLENE
Poor old dumpling.
Is she okay?

HADARA
Who knows?

DARLENE
We've been having awful security problems with our sliding glass door.

HADARA
I'm getting married on Friday to that Arab.

DARLENE
Sex can be beautiful, if it's with someone who knows what he's doing.

HADARA
He asked for a certificate of my virginity.

DARLENE
I fell in love with an Arab once when I was seventeen.
His Lebanese parents forbid him to see me.

HADARA
Because you're Jewish?

DARLENE
It wasn't because I'm Greek.
Hey, I look Greek, don't I?

HADARA
Didn't they know Arabs and Jews shared a common ancestor eight thousand years ago?

DARLENE
Maybe they realized the genes were either too close, or my blondeness comes from Jewish men marrying German or Slavic women a thousand years ago when they couldn't find enough women coming out of the Middle East to marry in those Rhineland villages.

HADARA
Am I your best friend?

DARLENE
We're both Litvaks.

HADARA
Maybe it's better to marry outside our diaspora.
Besides, I'm too American and too intellectual to think of myself as some word that sounds foreign.

DARLENE
There's cake in the fridge.
I'm going to work on my college term papers.

HADARA
Wait, we have to talk about the how the present changes our own futures based
on decisions we make right now.

DARLENE
My advice is not to marry him. Find a nice Jewish boy.
Such a choice will change your grandchildren's lives for all the generations.

HADARA
Like your dad?

DARLENE
Go to a Beverly Hills synagogue. Move there.
Give your babies a chance.

HADARA
With what? My college loan?
Do you want to give me a day job?

DARLENE
All you're going to meet in New York are Puerto Rican shipping clerks.
Nice Jewish boys won't marry you.

HADARA
Even with my master's degree in English?

DARLENE
No, because it's not a terminal degree.
What are you going to do, read them Shakespeare?

HADARA
Sounds like I'm auditioning for a soul mate.

DARLENE
They'll ask what your father does for a living.
They want your dad to set them up in business.
Or pay their medical school tuition.
You don't have big breasts and a small nose.

In fact, your face is scarred horribly.
So you'd better have daddy's big trust fund.
You have to be practical with men.

HADARA
I'd rather run my own business.
I'm marrying to get away from poverty.
Why do men ask what does your father do for a living instead of what you plan to do with your life?

DARLENE
Women are judged by what their husbands do.

HADARA
My dad mops toilets in the Navy Yard.
I'm too phobic to learn to drive.
And I don't feel safe alone with men.

DARLENE
Maybe you'll like being a bag lady.
You'll get to ride the stinky bus all your life.
What if I don't find a husband with a house as big as my dad's?

HADARA
There's a shortage of princes.
I'm desperate, Darlene, desperate.

DARLENE
My sister's already a producer in Beverly Hills.

HADARA
She graduated from an Ivy League drama school. You just started secretarial college.

DARLENE
Think a man cares what you do for a living? No one ever asked me what I do.

HADARA
All they ask me is what does your father do?

DARLENE
Your knight in armor wouldn't want you to neglect his babies.

HADARA
Or clean up after his horse.

DARLENE
What's your trade-off?
Without a doctorate, you'll never find a tenured job in academia.
I know because I work as a secretary for a college.

HADARA
I've already published a novel.

DARLENE
In a woman, that's like being a cripple.
Like I said, sooner or later, I'll get this big house.
My sister's already got the big script editing job in Hollywood.
Creative but poor gals like you need to stick with a real job like mine.

HADARA
Never. I need the Pulitzer Prize.
The road ahead lies in observing this planet.
We're news because we're the media.

DARLENE
And still waiting to be rescued, like the censored media.
So how do I launch you?

HADARA
I'm gifted, damn it. The media is an eternal teenager.

DARLENE
Don't think you're somebody special because you work hard. I work smart.

HADARA
When's the last time you ever shoveled snow?

DARLENE
Your brother's a lawyer why didn't he ever introduce you to his rich friends?

HADARA
Law is no profession for a poor boy.

DARLENE
My family would never turn their back on me.
But your brother hates you.

HADARA
Ignores. Fears. Withdraws.

DARLENE
You mom's retarded.

HADARA
She's a storefront musician, a psychic and a telepathic clairvoyant, like me.

DARLENE
She's a kvetch.

HADARA
Quality men freak out when they meet me.

DARLENE
Because you're bizarre. And I've heard that line enough from you.

HADARA
Your bust is as flat as mine.
So how come you're rich?

DARLENE
I had a nose job.

End of Scene.
Curtain.

Act III

New Scene: Spot Light/Sound Effects or CUT TO:

Tsipke's Apartment—Sept. 1963—Night

HADARA is sitting at her desk in her room reading a book on archaeology. The phone rings. She walks into the living room to answer it. She's alone at home.

HADARA
Hello? Oh, hi, Darlene.

DARLENE
(on phone)
My two-hundred dollar purse is missing.
I'm giving you a chance to return it before I phone the insurance company.

HADARA
You're crazy. I wouldn't touch your purse and ruin my reputation.

DARLENE
My mom's on the extension.

HADARA
Didn't you just come from your therapist?

DARLENE
Are you going to return my hundred and twenty-five dollar purse?
I'm calling the insurance company—now.

HADARA
I didn't see any purse.
But I can see from where you grabbed the idea.

On a separate phone line:

GOLDIE, (DARLENE'S MOTHER)
dials up HADARA's brother, BENJAMIN who's working late at his law office.

GOLDIE
Listen to this, you thief.

BENJAMIN
(on phone line)
Law Offices.
Hello? Is anyone on the line?

GOLDIE
Your mother was arrested for shoplifting.
What kind of a *forblundget* family are you, anyway?

BENJAMIN
What kind of trash?
Human garbage!
Are you trying to get me fired?

BENJAMIN makes angry gestures and hangs up on her.

HADARA
What I told you about my mom was in confidence.

DARLENE
Did you hear what my mom said?

HADARA
Who can I trust with my life?
Surely not my best friend.

DARLENE
There wasn't anyone else here.
HADARA
My own family scares me to hell.

GOLDIE
Darlene never lies to me.

HADARA
She's jealous of my Arab fiancé, because her own Arab boyfriend rejected your Jewish background.

GOLDIE
If you don't return her purse, I'll have your brother disbarred.
I'm making a citizen's arrest.

HADARA
Nothing can scare me any more.

DARLENE
Well, the next step is to tell the insurance company.

HADARA
You've never confided in me the way I've opened up to you.

DARLENE
You must have actually thought you were my best friend.

HADARA
I pity your real sister.

DARLENE
Like mother, like daughter.

HADARA
I'm the most honest person you'll ever meet.

DARLENE
Give him up, for your own sake.

HADARA
I'm marrying that Syrian.

GOLDIE
Don't waste your time.
Your children will be afraid to tell anyone from their father's country that you're Jewish.

HADARA bangs the receiver with a vengeance.

End of Scene. Curtain.

New Scene.

Curtain Rises:

October 25, 1963

Ext. Tsipke's Apartment House Brooklyn Day

HADARA and AHMED walk up the stairs.
They hold hands.
We see wedding ring on HADARA'S finger.
Couple is smiling. HADARA giggles.

AHMED
You tell your parents first.

HADARA
No, you tell my mom.

HADARA knocks on the door of her parent's apartment.
TSIPKE opens the door and smiles.

End of Scene. Curtain.

New Scene.

INT. TSIPKE'S APARTMENT BROOKLYN 8 DAY

TSIPKE
Come on in.
I was just soaking my bridges.

HADARA and AHMED walk in and sit down on the sofa.

HADARA
Mom, we were married two hours ago in the County Clerk's office.

TSIPKE
You're kidding?

AHMED
No. We did it.
We had a hard time finding two witnesses to sign the certificate.

TSIPKE
It's a good thing you didn't ask me to come down to city hall.
My angina has gotten so painful, that I can't walk out of the house at all these days.

HADARA
We found this couple who were waiting to be married.
They acted as our witnesses.

TSIPKE
MEIR, hey, cockroach back, flat butt, get in here.

MEIR staggers from his bedroom to the living room.

MEIR
Well, hello strangers.

TSIPKE
Those two just got married.

AHMED
(with an Arabic accent)
We're going to spend the night at the Americana Hotel.

HADARA
Yeah. And I'm paying the sixty dollars a day from my college loan money.

AHMED
I'm going to look for work if I can borrow three dollars from you.

HADARA
Now, he tells me, after we were married that he's not an engineer.

TSIPKE
How much can you hope to make?

AHMED
I'm a machinist. I'm looking for a job. I don't have a secondary school diploma.

TSIPKE
Where's Benjamin.
We need a lawyer.

HADARA
Benjamin doesn't care.

MEIR
What kind of schooling do you have?

AHMED
I left Syria at seventeen to learn to be a machinist in German factories.

HADARA
That's all he does, mom.
He's just a factory Joe.

TSIPKE
Do you want to stay married?

HADARA
Yes. He told me he wants to have his own business.

TSIPKE
Can't Benjamin help you?

HADARA
He kind of slithered away.

MEIR
Benjamin is starving.
He won't work for anybody, and he can't find clients.

HADARA
Benjamin is dying with diabetes.
Don't bother him, I warn you.

TSIPKE
Well, before you go to the hotel, I want to give you a present.

TSIPKE scurries into the kitchen and grabs a gift-wrapped package from the cupboard.

AHMED
Is that a gift for me?

TSIPKE
I knew you two were going to be married soon.

TSIPKE hands the gift-wrapped package to AHMED.
He takes it and smiles, unwrapping it.

AHMED
Thank you, momma.

A dozen packages of condoms fall out of the package.
AHMED is startled.
HADARA breaks out in laughter.
She can't stop laughing.
AHMED examines one condom carefully, reading the package label.

AHMED
(laughing)
I thought you were giving me a wedding present, you know, like a watch.

HADARA
You knew we were going on our honeymoon tonight.

TSIPKE
My psychic abilities never fail me.

AHMED
Thank you, mommy.

TSIPKE
Don't let him put the rubber on dry and then ram into you.
That's how your old man tore me apart.

MEIR
Oh, shut your face.
I didn't know about women.

TSIPKE
He ripped me open trying to jam a dry condom into a young virgin.

MEIR
Is that why you made such an ugly, cringing face the first time?
I thought it was because I didn't take a bath.

TSIPKE
It was all over before you entered me.
Ahmed, he's a premature ejaculator. Hope you're not.

HADARA
Ma, don't embarrass him.

AHMED
We really must go.

TSIPKE
Where you eating dinner?

AHMED
Chinese restaurant.

MEIR
Go, already. It's six o'clock.

TSIPKE
(winking)
Gee, you made me feel young again.
I feel like it was me going on my honeymoon with a new man.

MEIR
Tsipke is watching our marriage die.

TSIPKE
Well, you're not pumping anything into it.
Our marriage is still just like I wrote on my honeymoon on that train to Florida.

MEIR
I remember finding your diary and crying. You wrote "Today I died."

TSIPKE
The real 'me' did. You only see what my job, my responsibility is. To take care of all of you, but it's like an observer from above looking down on a body going through the motions of taking care of you while my 'real' days of fun and adventure slip away as if I were invisible. We're all invisible and so totally alone.

HADARA
I'll be at the Americana for two days.

TSIPKE
So, long, honey. Hope you can still walk.

End of Scene.
Curtain.

NEW YEAR'S EVE, 1969

FADE IN:

INT. BALLROOM OF PLUSH HOTEL AT NIGHT

A live band is playing. A Hawaiian buffet is set out.
Couples are dancing. There is a Christmas tree.
Music plays "Auld Lang Syne."

HADARA (28) and AHMED (32) are seated at a table with untouched plates of food in front of them.

AHMED
You're too crazy to have a lawyer.

HADARA
Why are you sending my babies to Syria?

AHMED
My mother will raise them just like I was raised.

HADARA
Answer my question.

AHMED
Just tell my lawyer that your health is too bad.

HADARA
But you told me if I signed the house over to you, that the divorce would be canceled.
Is this supposed to be the perfect marriage? I was always told that old proverb: that it's better to be lucky than rich.

AHMED
It costs too much to bring up kids here. Besides, they'd grow up to be drug addicts or whores...like American kids.

HADARA
You can't take them.
Please let me have just one.

AHMED
I'm not separating my kids.
They're my life. You can finally have that career.
Isn't that what you really want?

HADARA
I want a career for the time when my children will be busy with their own lives.
Besides, I paid thirty dollars for this romantic dinner.

AHMED
I want to be rid of you.
You're a stone around my neck. I want to be free.

HADARA
You want to be free?
There's no man freer than you.

AHMED
It's midnight.
I've got to get back to my restaurant.

At midnight, the music grows louder, all the couples sitting and on the dance floor hung and kiss.

HADARA
I can't stand to be alone in that mice-infested house.

AHMED
You want money?
Then go out and earn it.
Get a job like I had to do.

HADARA
I gave up that option when you forced me to have children.

AHMED gives HADARA the "barber's itch."
He pinches the hair at the nape of her neck and pulls her hair upwards to give her a sharp pain.
HADARA screams.

AHMED
Lower your voice, your whore.
Didn't you hear me? I said lower your voice.
I'll beat the sassiness out of you.

HADARA
That belly dancer told me you're the worst lover she ever had.

AHMED grabs HADARA and shakes her.
He throws her to the floor and kicks her as the dancing couples watch in horror.

AHMED
Are you coming home?

HADARA
How come your whore is old enough to be my mother?

AHMED
You're going to get it later tonight, you bitch.

End of Scene. Lights Out

New Scene at Hadara's Modest Cottage In San Diego:

Ext. Hadara's Modest Cottage.

Ahmed Shoves Hadara Up The Driveway And Into The House.

Int. Living Room Hadara's Home Night

She flops down on the sofa. AHMED paces the living room floor circling around her like a beast.

HADARA
I'm a total romantic.

AHMED hurries to the desk drawer and retrieves his handgun. He puts the gun in HADARA'S head.

AHMED
I want custody of the kids or you'll be dead in twenty-four hours.

AHMED shoves her back on the sofa as she tries to rise. He turns around, waving the gun, and thrusts his buttocks in HADARA'S face.

AHMED
Why do you think I go with a woman ten years older than you?
See any tail up there, man-hater?

HADARA
(shoves him away)
Get your butt out of my face.
She probably makes you feel important, and I make you feel responsible.

AHMED
I'm a man, not a beast.
No? No horns? No tail?

AHMED spins around and puts the gun in her head again.

HADARA
Your favorite pick-me-up is putting me down.

AHMED puts the gun in his belt and lights a cigarette. He rips off his shirt and lifts his arm, rubbing out the lighted cigarette in his armpit.

AHMED
See these scars?
What must I do to get rid of the pain?

AHMED rolls up his sleeveless undershirt to reveal shrapnel scars on his torso.

HADARA
I've seen them before.

AHMED
I'm willing to die…to kill to preserve the honor of my babies.

HADARA
And you're sending my kids back to Syria where twice you were tortured in jail there?

AHMED
The morals of too many Americans are like pigs.

AHMED spits in HADARA's face.

HADARA
Why'd you bring your two brothers here to live with us? I'm like a white slave.

AHMED
I'm running a restaurant, not a whorehouse.

HADARA
I gave up a Jewish doctor for you, just to make peace.

AHMED
Peace? You think you're too good for me?
You think you're some pampered princess.
Don't you know anything about the care of husbands?
Bitch. Why'd you marry me?

HADARA
So I'd have a good subject for a book or a movie.
I wanted to be a visual anthropologist.
I couldn't afford the tuition.
So I decided to live as the other half lives in the third world.
I wanted to understand what it feels like to be an Arab.

AHMED
I'm not good enough for you, am I?

HADARA
You destroyed me.

AHMED
Look at you...a lawyer for a brother.
Your father's a janitor...mops toilets at night.
Eight-grade education...
I own my own business.
And I never graduated from secondary school.

HADARA
You need street smarts to compete.

AHMED
I dropped out of school to work as a machinist.

AHMED shakes her.

HADARA
Didn't I lease that restaurant and get you started in business?
Did I leave you when I found out you lied?
Doctor of mechanical engineering, bullshine.

AHMED
You're no good as a mother or as a woman.

HADARA
What kind of a father would dump his kids on his mother?
In another country, yet?
And then go back to his restaurant?

AHMED
Hamed, get your tail in here.

HADARA
How come you always run out of words?
Then your fists fly.
I'm a rich girl without money.
Not a poor girl.

AHMED
I want a divorce.
You're a rope around my neck.
I want to be free.

HADARA
Then give others freedom.
I'm housebound with panic disorder.
You're penniless.
What a great time to ask for a divorce.

AHMED
Hamed. Hurry up.
I need you in here.

AHMED calls in his brother, HAMED. He wakes up and treks into the living room, sleepy. He smiles a broad, weird grin, and looks at HADARA sadistically. AHMED presses the sharp edge of the oriental coffee pot on the living room table against the side of HADARA'S head.

AHMED motions for his brother's help. HAMED walks over the HADARA. HAMED laughs wildly. The two men exchange words in Arabic.

HAMED pulls HADARA to her feet by her wrists. AHMED and HAMED drag HADARA into the bathroom and AHMED dips HADARA'S head into the toilet bowl and flushes.

AHMED
How many times have I told you to scrub the bowl?

HAMED
(laughing weirdly)
She never cleans it after somebody sprays the bowl with diarrhea.

AHMED drags HADARA'S head out of the flushing water by her hair.

AHMED
Hand me my razor blade.

HAMED fetches the straight razor from the cabinet and holds it. AHMED holds HADARA by the hair with one hand while she cries and screams and takes the razor in his other hand from HAMED.

HAMED
Shut your trap.
The neighbors will hear.

AHMED holds HADARA's wrists together in one hand with his steely strength while he presses the straight razor against both her wrists. HADARA trembles and sobs.

AHMED
If you try to fight me for custody in this divorce,
I'll slash your wrists and then tell the police you committed suicide.

HADARA
Don't leave me while I'm still agoraphobic.
I'll give you my parent's apartment house.

AHMED
Go unlock the door, Hamed.

HAMED drags HADARA across the living room floor by the wrists.
AHMED helps him. HAMED laughs. AHMED spits in HADARA'S face again.
He pulls her women's liberation emblem from the wall and kicks it along the carpet.

AHMED holds the razor against her throat and looks her in the eye for one long, silent moment. Then he throws HADARA out of the door into the night. It is raining. Spotlight or angle on AHMED on the telephone.

AHMED
Police? I want to report my wife has tried to commit suicide again.
Hurry over here. My two kids are sleeping, and I don't want her back in here to upset them.

Curtain. Lights Out:
End of Scene

New Scene
Curtain Rises:

Ext. Hadara's Home Rainy Night

HADARA bangs on the door. She cries, sobs, screams. But no one answers. She slithers down the door and sits in a heap on the doorstep as the rain washes over her.

Ext. Next Door Neighbor's House Night

HADARA sidles over to the next-door neighbor. She rings the bell. AVA JOHNSON, a young housewife answers.

AVA
Hey, it's three o'clock in the morning.

HADARA
He threw me out.
Can I come in?

AVA
Look, I don't want to get involved.

HADARA
Please…

Int. Ava Johnson's Living Room Night

AVA
So he tossed you on your ear again.
A woman is nothing without a real man.

HADARA
A woman without a man can go to bed knowing she'll still be alive in the morning.

AVA
You killed your own marriage.
Don't think I didn't hear it die.

HADARA
He didn't pump anything into it.

AVA
Woman, you're addicted to romance.
I bet you read all those romance novels.

HADARA
Read them? I write them.

AVA
So what are you here for?

HADARA
My psychiatrist betrayed me.
He played the recorded tapes of our session to my husband.
He's Ahmed's friend.
Ahmed is keeping his rugs for him in his restaurant.
My doctor betrayed me after he promised me what I said would be confidential.

AVA
What do you expect?
You just said that the doctor is his best friend.

HADARA
I don't have any friends, and no living relatives.
I feel I'm in the way between your husband and you.

AVA
I'm not your friend.
I'm your neighbor.

HADARA
Ava, help me.

AVA
I can't help you.
You can probably attract men, but you'll never keep them.

HADARA
He expects me to go out and find a job.
I don't want to work. I want a man to support me so
I can fulfill my career dreams.

AVA
Tough luck, cookie.
Fulfill your dreams after sixty-five like I'll have to do.

HADARA
I'm agoraphobic.
There's no way I can walk out of that house.

AVA
Love junkie! He's already kicked you to mediocrity.
Girl, do you have a sense of entitlement to cure?

End of Scene
Curtain

New Scene
Curtain Rises:

December 22, 1971

Int. Hadara's Furnished Room Nearly Dawn

There's a knock on the door.
HADARA crawls out of her studio sofa bed to answer it.
AHMED stands before her holding her two children, FAWZI, a boy of four, and SAMIRA, a girl of five. The children are dressed lavishly.

HADARA
Is it time for them to go already?

HADARA runs to her desk and brings two gifts for the children.

AHMED
Why'd you have to go and buy them such bulky toys to take on the plane.

FAWZI and SAMIRA squeal and jump for joy, unwrapping their toys.

HADARA
You're still not going with them?

AHMED
The airline's hostess will get them to Syria alone.

HADARA
My kids are only four and five years old.

AHMED
My kids.

HADARA
Really?
Want to see my two episiotomies scars?

AHMED
Fawzi, Samira, kiss your mother goodbye.

HADARA
I want to get a last look at a percentage of my genes.

AHMED
Hurry it up.

HADARA
My daughter, promise me that you'll marry a rich doctor if you can't be one yourself.

AHMED
Don't make her American.

HADARA
American citizenship was my greatest gift to you.

AHMED
You're a crazy woman.

HADARA
Is that your excuse for never offering me a dime of community property?
You're disappearing with all the money from the sale of your restaurant.

HADARA looks up at AHMED's face. He spits on her wall-hanging, a women's liberation sign of the new feminist movment—a female sign—(Venus hieroglyph) with a fist. The children observe his actions.

AHMED
You still get panic attacks, don't you?

HADARA
Mr. Hostility, you just created the new poor.
I'll remember you as the take-away-man.

AHMED
Go ahead. Make yourself rich.
I came to this country with fifty dollars in my wallet.

HADARA
And you're leaving me in a man's world with two shiny quarters.

AHMED shuffles the two children out the door and slams it behind him. Dawn comes up through the curtains.
HADARA hops back into bed and turns up her small radio to "CANON in D" classical music.
The phone rings.

HADARA
Yes?

HODA
(on telephone line)
This is your ex-husband's whore.

HADARA
What the hell do you want from me, Hoda?

HODA
I think you're the most selfish bitch that ever walked.
How could you give up your children?
Because you're too lazy to support them?

HADARA
You're being illogical.
There's no way you or anyone else can ever make me feel pain again.

HODA
I'd kill before I'd turn my kids over to my ex.

HADARA
No you wouldn't.
Do me a favor. Tell me why I keep marrying toxic people?

HADARA bangs the receiver on the holder and sobs hysterically. HADARA turns up the music louder as the soft waves of "CANON in D" bring a calmness to the dawn and the silent, lonely room.

Curtain.
End of Scene. New Scene.

Christmas Eve, 1971

Ext. Synagogue Night

HADARA walks up the stairs for the Friday night Sabbath service.
Int. Synagogue Social Hall Night

The service is over and the buffet dessert table is laden with tea and cakes.
HADARA takes a plate with cheese cake and a cup of tea.
She looks up to see BRONNA GREEN, 36, smile at her.

BRONNA
Balmy night for Christmas Eve and Hannukah.

HADARA
Hi. I'm Hadara.
Are you alone?

BRONNA
Bronna Green.
Just divorced. You too?

HADARA nods affirmatively.

BRONNA
You look it.
If we're not feeling good about ourselves, we'll marry the man who'll reflect our low self esteem of the moment.

HADARA
How true.
What did yours do for a living?

BRONNA
I put him through medical school.

HADARA
At least you got to be a doctor's wife.
I always dreamed of being a doctor's wife.

BRONNA
Yeah, well a lot of 'em don't want you to have your own career.
And they all want children. You have to kiss their butt. Then they
Dump you for a younger, healthier woman when you get old and sick before your time.

HADARA
How your mother felt about herself, that determines whom you'll marry.
Tell me about yourself.
How on earth did a short, small-breasted woman like you get a doctor to marry you?
Did you have a rich father?

BRONNA
Yes. He's a well-known builder in San Francisco. And I'm just finishing my master's in marriage counseling.

HADARA
It figures. Were you valuable as a kid?

BRONNA
My dad dealt with seductiveness by acting distant.

HADARA
And you found out men are not available.

BRONNA
Hey, you're a regular therapist.

HADARA
Yeah…kind of…I write fiction.

BRONNA
Are you attracted to cold men?

HADARA
Silver-plated robots! I'm a science fiction nut, robots, aliens, and the works.

BRONNA
Ghostly lovers, eh?

HADARA
You make money playing out old conflicts?

BRONNA
No man will ever live up to my father. I keep my distance from men.

HADARA
At least you're out of a toxic relationship.

BRONNA
And what are you doing to select a certain type of man?

BRONNA and HADARA move along the buffet line, chatting, while people bend over to listen to their conversation. They pile their plates high with sweets.

HADARA
Women who hate me for tooting my own horn spread the word in public that I'm a man hater. They love writing that in the media. I'm not, though. I'm looking for a daddy to love me. What do you say we dump the sweets? Want to come to my place for a vegetable spread and talk practical?

BRONNA pauses to consider, then smiles and nods.
The two women head for HADARA'S furnished room.

EXT. BRONNA gets in her car. HADARA enters car.

HADARA
I never learned to drive.
Give me a lift two miles?

BRONNA
Why can't you drive?

HADARA
I inherited the fear gene from my dad.

BRONNA motions for her to hop in.

BRONNA
Never mind. Hop in. There's only one way to choose a husband.
Find out how quickly a man gets angry, before you marry.

HADARA offers BRONNA a firm handshake. She accepts it, smiling.

HADARA
I put a husband-wanted ad in the daily newspaper.

BRONNA
Any response?

HADARA
Fourteen letters, since yesterday.

Curtain
End of Scene

Act Three

Next Scene
Curtain Rises

July 1985

Ext. Hadara's Low Rent Cottage Dusk

HADARA'S modest stucco cottage stands in a poor, multi-racial neighborhood where swarms of shouting children play in the gutter.

INT. HADARA'S HOME DUSK

The entire living room and HADARA's bedroom and den are covered with photographs and posters of Mr. Spock (of Star Trek).

Star Trek fan material covers the walls of the den of the tiny three-bedroom cottage.

In the den, HADARA's desk is strewn with science fiction paperbacks and magazines. The bookcase is filled with paperback Star Trek Novels.
A giant poster of Mr. Spock is plastered in the wall of HADARA's den where she sits keyboarding at her personal computer.

Manuscripts are piled on her desk. We see her finishing the typing of the last page of a screenplay. Her tape recorder/stereo is playing the baroque classical music.
Spotlight or angle on HADARA's face as she looks up at Mr. Spock's poster/picture above her computer.

HADARA
Don't you know you're the right man for me because you'll always be unattainable? So will all my ghost lovers from previous lives in different countries. So will the richest man in ancient Rome and Greece.

The phone rings. HADARA picks it up. There's loud static at the other end. Silence. She's about to bang down the receiver when a voice breaks through from a distance.

HADARA
Hello?
Well, speak up.

FAWZI
Mommy?

HADARA
My son, David Joseph?
Oh that's right.
He changed your name.
What's your name now?

FAWZI
This is Fawzi Mohammed.
My father used to be married to you.
This is your son.

HADARA
Where are you?

FAWZI
Syria.

HADARA
This is the first time I've heard from you in sixteen years.

FAWZI
I've kept your picture since I was four years old.

HADARA
Holy Toledo! Oh, for heaven's sake.
My kid. Where's your sister?

FAWZI
At her girl friend's house.

HADARA
When can I see you?

FAWZI
Mommy, help me.
I need five hundred dollars to come to America.
That's the only way I can finish my studies in physics.

HADARA
Yes. I'll help. But I don't have a cent.
My second husband gives me fifty dollars a week for food.

FAWZI
Can I come to live with you?

HADARA
My house is too small. I don't know what to do.

FAWZI
I'm coming to see you.

HADARA
Okay. I'll ask my husband to kick out the tenant from his rental.

FAWZI
What do you look like?

HADARA
White hair, bags under my eyes, and lots of wrinkles.

FAWZI
I'll call you when I arrive.

The phone clicks off.

HADARA
Hello? Hello?
Is anybody on the line?

HADARA leaps for joy and plants a kiss on the poster of Mr. Spock. Then HADARA runs to her second husband's bedroom.
(They have always shared separate rooms.)
HADARA pauses, and then knocks on his door.

ERIC
Better make it quick, I'm real busy.

In his room, ERIC AUER is busy soldering circuit boards on the computer he's building. It's his hobby. ERIC'S tape recorder is playing old time radio comedy. Soft music is wafting.

HADARA
Hey, most distant man in the galaxy, it's important.

ERIC
Tune me out, kid.
Don't bug me.

HADARA
I have to talk to you.
Come on and give me a hug.

ERIC
Not this week. I'm beat.

HADARA
My son called from Syria.

ERIC
Oh, give me a break.

HADARA
Not until you give me a connection.

ERIC
Would you stop arguing?

HADARA
This is my normal conversational voice.

ERIC
I bet you'll be excited to see them.
When are they coming?

HADARA
Soon.
They need a place to live.

ERIC
You must be excited after sixteen years of no correspondence.

HADARA
You have to kick the tenant out.

ERIC
Why can't you sleep on the sofa?
You'd better give them your bedroom.

HADARA
Oh, no. You're not going to kick me out of my room for them.
That's what my brother did when he got married.
He could have rented an apartment.

ERIC
You're not going to let your kids see this roach-filled dump, are you?

HADARA
Who cares?

ERIC
I'm too ashamed to let them see what a lousy housekeeper you are.
What a loser.
Do they know you're a phobic who failed her driver's test nine times?

HADARA
Why do you always take my choices away?

ERIC
All you ever wanted was to be taken care of like Cinderella.

HADARA
There's a shortage of princes, so I married an angry man.
I married a man who has been impotent only with me for decades.
Why have I given up love for money that never materializes?

ERIC
You're the new age Cinderella.

HADARA
The only thing I'll inherit is my own wisdom.

ERIC
Your kids will never tell you their business.
All you'll hear is their bad news.

HADARA
They're more worried that I won't keep my mouth shut.

ERIC
I'll have to carry two big mortgages alone.
Who's going to pay the mortgage on our other house, you?

HADARA
What'll they think when I tell them I'm Jewish?

ERIC
They're devout Moslems from Syria.
What do you think?

End of Scene. Curtain

Curtain Rises, New Scene:

Summer. The Present

Int. Hadara's Living Room Night

SAMIRA, HADARA'S daughter, 21, walks into HADARA'S living room.
The two women embrace.
FAWZI, 20, follows behind and gives his mother a big hug.
He resembles her.

HADARA
Sit down. I've laid out a buffet of fruit and veggies.

SAMIRA
What does your husband do?

HADARA
He's a pool of anger.
Eric repairs equipment, like computers and gadgets.
He's a blue-collar Joe, and I've learned not to cringe when I say it.

SAMIRA
My father's a very rich man in Syria.

ERIC
Oh? Then why can't he pay me rent?

HADARA
You look exactly like my mother.
I guess she reincarnated.

SAMIRA
I'm marrying a doctor next month.
He's coming here from Syria.

HADARA
Gee, I always wanted to marry a doctor since I was ten.
No such luck in New York finding a doctor to marry, though.
How come you married a doctor? You look just like me.

FAWZI
My father told us you are a doctor.

HADARA
Oh, no. I write science fiction scripts and novels.
But I haven't ever earned a dime.

ERIC
Does your father have a job?

FAWZI
No. He was arrested as a spy, put in prison in Syria, and was beaten until he became a mental vegetable. I need to live with him. I can't live alone here. You see when he went back to Syria, the people in the government said he married an American Jewess. They took away all his money.

ERIC
Do you cook?

SAMIRA
No, the servants chased me out of the kitchen.

FAWZI
She was raised like a princess.

HADARA
Did your father ever visit you?

SAMIRA
Twice. Once for two years.

HADARA
Where's your father now?

FAWZI
He was thrown in jail and tortured.
The doctor said he had schizophrenia.

ERIC
How awful for you.

HADARA
If only you had answered my letters or acknowledged my gifts, Eric would have adopted you fifteen years ago.

SAMIRA
Do you work for money?

HADARA
I'm a housewife. Want to make something of it?

ERIC
She's as much of a failure as I am.
Only she has a master's degree.
I dropped out of college and have a very short temper.

HADARA
Why don't you two eat something?

FAWZI and SAMIRA stare at the food but don't touch it. They shake their heads "no."

HADARA
We're vegan vegetarians.
You won't find pork or alcohol here.

ERIC
You're mother is Jewish.
Does that scare you?

FAWZI
Don't tell my Arab friends.
And don't tell my wife and children.

ERIC
And I'm English and German American.

SAMIRA
Are you Christian?

ERIC
I'm a spiritualist and medium.
Ever play the Ouija board?
You'd be surprised at the entities that come through.

HADARA
His mom brought him up Lutheran.
But we go to psychic séances.

SAMIRA
If you ever tell my husband or children that you're Jewish, I'll run away.
You'll never see me again.

HADARA
Take it easy.
May the life force expand to all the trillion universes.
Live long, rich, and healthy.

ERIC
I hate fanatics.

HADARA
You don't have to be human to eat Levi's rye bread.
Just dip it in Arabic hummos and tabbouli salad.
Why is it so difficult to enjoy my ambiguity or your diversity?

ERIC
Let's all join the Federation.
Your mom's a Trekkie who likes the Federation of Planets.

HADARA holds up a gold chain from which dangles a gold Star of David.

HADARA
It's a shame there's no one to pass my grandmother's Jewish star onto for the next generation.

ERIC
You made that choice when you married your children's father.

FAWZI
I'll take it.

FAWZI retrieves the necklace and puts it over his own head.

ERIC
See? He wears it under his shirt.
I bet it'll go into a box, and his Arab wife and kids will never see it.

SAMIRA
Don't let my children see it.
My husband knows all about you.

HADARA
So how come you got married and didn't invite me to the wedding?

SAMIRA
It was an Islamic ceremony.
All my Arabic real family and friends are going.

ERIC
You're a robot to them.
You're a stranger to everyone.

HADARA
Hey, kids, you're all the family I have.

ERIC
You're forgetting me.
Today's our anniversary.

FAWZI
How'd you meet him?

HADARA
He was the last letter to reply to my husband-wanted ad in the papers in 1974.

SAMIRA
And how'd he turn out?

HADARA
Look at Eric.
Listen to how he talks to me.

ERIC
Hey, show some respect, or I'll wash your mouth out with soap.

HADARA
I'm sorry. It's just that he keeps bellyaching.

ERIC
When are you going to make me rich?

HADARA
When you win the lottery.

The beeping of an automobile horn is heard.
SAMIRA leaps up and looks out the window.

SAMIRA
It's Abdo, my husband.

CURTAIN OR FADE OUT/LIGHTS OUT.

End of Scene.

NEW SCENE.

Int. Hadara's Bedroom, Same Night

ERIC
Well, your kids are grown, married, and have their own children, grandma.

HADARA
Are you sorry you had a vasectomy ten years before we met?

ERIC
No. I wouldn't want to pass on my genes for depression.

HADARA
A lot of good my high IQ did for me.

ERIC
You still have a superior mind drenched in inferior brain chemicals.

HADARA
If only I had those brains in a man's body, I could find a good income.

ERIC
If you're so smart, how come you don't have the secret of a happy marriage?
And how come you don't have any real job?
I see you're reading the care and feeding of Labrador Retrievers.
How about husbands?

HADARA
How about wives?
I'm smart enough to play at the work I love.

ERIC
Isn't it funny?
Nowadays, men want to be heroes and women want money.
Ten years ago men wanted sex, and women wanted love.

HADARA
We're alone and in deep decline at last in this house.
At last I have a nice backyard to do my Tai Chi Chuan.

ERIC
We're not alone in the universe.
Everybody's watching us.

ERIC looks up at the poster/picture of Mr. Spock on the wall of HADARA'S bedroom.

HADARA
I feel safe in his presence because he never gets angry.

ERIC
Safe?

HADARA
I have a right to verbalize my deepest feelings.
He won't chase me, shove me, or beat me.
Men never call me a man-hater.
Just women do, and only in print.

ERIC
All I can offer you is my impatience.

HADARA
You'll never admit you hit me.
Don't you remember doing it because I didn't like that old bookcase?
If you're my husband and friend, then who's my enemy?

ERIC
(grinning)
Only you, my love.

HADARA
You've put me down and hit me all these years.
It happens only when I state my needs.
If I'm silent all the time and smile, it never happens.

ERIC
If I can't be a hero to you, why stay for my money?
You will never get any of it.

HADARA
Then why do you want me to live here?
I don't have any other place to go.

ERIC
I'm not here to hit you.
The always door stays open if you want to leave.
You know we're not compatible and have nothing in common.

HADARA
Yes. I agree we have nothing in common.
We're not compatible.
But that doesn't mean I can't continue sleeping in my room.

ERIC
You can continue sleeping here in your room.

HADARA
You've never kissed me on the lips. Give me a hug.

ERIC
Not now. Ask me in a couple of weeks.

HADARA
I never felt safe with you.
Someday you will murder me, probably strangle me with a wire.

ERIC
Did you have to tell the kids our marriage never was consummated?

HADARA
Why not? I want them to know I gave up everything.

ERIC
I'm so embarrassed. That's like cutting off my manhood.

HADARA
You know when you'll kill me, Eric?
It will be when I demand respect.
I won't have to wait until I say I'm leaving.

ERIC
The subject is closed.

Eric walks away. She trails after him.

HADARA
You won't remember why you'd snapped.
Part of it will be to use anger to get power.
You're too much of a miser to hire someone like in the movie, "Midnight Lace."

ERIC
There's too much clutter on the kitchen counter.
When are you going to wash the floor?

HADARA
She asked why we have separate bedrooms and separate bank accounts.
From where'd you learn your knee-jerk hostility?

ERIC
We made a contract, a deal.

HADARA
It's a fair trade. You pay me food money to stay.
You won't even let me take care of my houseplants.
My main complaint is that you don't allow talking very often.

ERIC
Why the hell did an orthodox Jewish woman from Brooklyn marry a Middle Eastern revolutionary?

HADARA
I thought a drastic change from my dad's anger was necessary for happiness.

ERIC
(gruff concern)
Every woman gets the face and the man she deserves. Was it worth it?

HADARA
Jewish women marry Arab Sheiks when they want to talk with daddy.

ERIC
Maybe you need some religion. Seems you not only want a daddy, you want the Lord.

HADARA
Women usually marry men like their daddies or what's familiar.

End of Scene.

Curtains.

New Scene Curtain Rises On The Present Day In A Park Or Beach Setting.

Ext. Beach The Present Day

HADARA and ERIC are walking along the beach, side by side.
HADARA takes ERIC'S hand for a moment, but then he pulls away and walks faster so that for awhile he's walking ahead of her.

HADARA
Would you slow down?
I can't keep up with you.
You're always running ahead.

ERIC slows down and they walk side by side.
This time, ERIC takes HADARA's hand.

ERIC
My football coach made a pass at me when I was fifteen.
You're the only person I can tell this to.

HADARA
I've already accepted you as you are.
I'd be scared of anyone different.

ERIC
So we're both abused children who shelved the option for rearing kids.

HADARA
The biological clock has run out, and we're alone.
Why didn't I think of adoption years ago?
I couldn't replace my biological children.
Someday I always hoped they'd come back to me, like my runaway cat.

ERIC
Your kids never call you, not even on mother's day.

HADARA
What do you expect? They moved across the country.
They make the pilgrimage to Mecca each year, but California is too far for them to visit me.

ERIC stops at an ice cream stand on the beach.
HADARA follows and puts her arm around ERIC.

ERIC
Two snow cones, please.

ERIC fumbles in his wallet.

ERIC
Give me a dollar for yours.

HADARA
Here, miser.
You've never pay for me anytime we go out to eat.
But I swore I'd focus on the positive.

ERIC and HADARA walk away, eating their snow cones.

End of Scene Lights Out.

New Scene, Lights On or Brief Curtain.

Curtain Rises or Lights Come On.

Ext. Beach—The Present Summer at Sunset.

A fire is glowing in the beach fire ring.
HADARA and ERIC are toasting kebobs on skewers over the fire.
They are alone, gazing at the sunset on the beach.

ERIC
We've never gone out together to watch the sunset before.

HADARA
You were always building your computers in your bedroom with the door locked.

ERIC
And you?

HADARA
I created a whole world from my isolation.
People are such a pain in the butt, that solitude is heaven.

ERIC
That's the wages of selling your isolation to the movies.
Crowds in the media make their living from giving you recognition.

HADARA
Now that I'm rich, I can look for Mister Right.
Only he'll be waiting for the bedpan in a nursing home.

ERIC
Will you dump me?
I'm in great shape.

HADARA
No. You've danced away decades ago.
And I'm too comfortable in my little house.
Every time change comes, you find an excuse to hit me.

ERIC
Did I ever ask you what you were when I met you?

HADARA
No. You never cared what ethnic group I chose as my core identity.
See, I don't inherit a core identity.
I choose it out of fear.
How come I see you watching all those old Nazi marching films on TV?
And you like blondes!
You like what you look like.
You're blonde, and I have dark hair. So why is it important to you?

ERIC
'Cause it's my core identity, and I did inherit it.
First you married a man who tried to put his fist through your belly button the day before you gave birth.
Why?
Because you spent six hundred dollars in a month on food.
Boy, what a worthless loser you are.
That's why people don't want to be around you.

HADARA
So you blame the victim.
I married a man with a knee-jerk blame-the-victim personality.
My next mistake was telling you the details of my first marriage.

ERIC
How else can I teach you to stop *playing* the victim?
That's enough of your arguing.

HADARA
You'll always be a blue collar Joe. I'll always love the opera.
I want to kosher my kitchen and listen to music.
It will distract me from my real problems—your abuse and my declining body.

ERIC
Stop using your grandparent's religion as an excuse. What do you really want?

HADARA
I'd like a dream house with central heat and a subscription to *Architectural Digest.*
Home and Garden's passed me by.

ERIC
Will you leave me when you make more money than I do?

HADARA
No. We made a fair trade.

ERIC
Do you still dream of Mister Right—your soul mate?

HADARA
It has been always your house—never our house.
How safe could my house be?

ERIC
What you really needed was to put two empty chairs down.
Then have a long talk with your dad's spirit.
In the next world, the angry are tame.

HADARA
I can't take care of myself.
The man I married can't take care of a wife.

ERIC
You're describing your dad and your first husband again.
What was it like posing as an Arab housewife for seven years in the middle of a
Brooklyn Jewish ghetto—and knowing you're really Jewish?

HADARA
It was more exciting than being nine years old and having my father chase me
through the cellar with an ax in one hand and a hammer in the other.

HADARA and ERIC eat the food as they watch the sun set below the horizon.

ERIC
Was it worth it?

HADARA
The men in my life were all stick figures, cave drawings.

ERIC
How could you stand to be discriminated against as an Arab in New York and beaten for looking Jewish in New Jersey?

HADARA
I finally found a core identity that nobody discriminates against—Early New England settler.

ERIC
That's my family background....here in America since the sixteen hundreds.

HADARA
We're married. So what's yours is now mine.

ERIC
The whole third world discriminates against my core identity.

HADARA
Well name one core identity that I can choose that everybody loves.

ERIC
You can't please everyone. Just be yourself.

HADARA
Why can't everybody love me with my core identity?

ERIC
Try giving of yourself.
It's time to be happy

HADARA
I am happy.
What's left after happiness?
Escape or an extreme make-over?

ERIC
Why did you marry me? Didn't you like yourself enough?

HADARA
I put an ad in the papers for a man slow to anger.
Then I married you.
Oh, boy.
I should have dated you years longer.

ERIC
Well, I played you my astrologer's tape on our second date.
You saw my horoscope.
She said I was very quick to anger.

HADARA
And I let that statement slip by me.

ERIC
Why did you agree to marry me?

HADARA
You asked me to move into your apartment.
I was homeless and knew you only six weeks.

ERIC
Wasn't there chemistry? Were you that desperate?

HADARA
I was homeless and penniless when my ex tossed me out the door.

ERIC
You could have worked a few years after your divorce.

HADARA
I guess I forgot to ask your mother, relatives, or friends.
There were warning signals.
You didn't visit your mother often.
Your military father put you down.
And you banked your anger into a pool
Then you spent your stress on me.

ERIC
Neither of us have any friends.
That's all we have in common.

HADARA
I'm tired of absorbing your frustration like a sponge.

ERIC
Everyone liked me at work for all those years.

HADARA
Your co-worker's only saw your public mask.
It was the same charm my first husband used on his customers.

ERIC
Really, why did you marry me?

HADARA
I thought Anglo-Saxon husbands never raised their voices at home.

The phone rings. HADARA rushes to pick it up.

HADARA
Yes. This is she.
Oh, hello.
Well, thank you.
I'm eternally grateful.
Sure. I'll wait for the contract in the mail.

HADARA hangs up lightly. She leaps into the air screaming and laughing with joy.

ERIC
What happened?

HADARA
I've made you rich, you ingrate.
That producer just bought my movie and novel in a package deal.

ERIC
Oh, my God. I'm so proud of you.

ERIC rushes over and gives her a hug.

HADARA
I've waited for this moment for years.

ERIC
I suspected you could do it, against all odds of age discrimination.

HADARA
I can buy my dream house now, and get rid of this Salvation Army furniture.

ERIC
Maybe I'll take you to eat at the soup and salad place.

HADARA
You've never allowed me to have feelings.
Neither did my ex or my dad.

ERIC
You're too much like me.
Go boot up your computer.
And I'll boot up mine.
We'll write to each other from opposite ends of the house.

HADARA
Remember on our wedding night?
You watched the football game on TV all evening.
Then you fell asleep without even a hug. And snored so loud.

ERIC
Well at least on our first three dates we had fun.

HADARA
That's what happens when you shack up for a year before the wedding.
Familiarity breeds disinterest.

ERIC
The door's open. You're free to leave anytime if you don't like it here.

HADARA
Where would I go? My income is only as good as my last book or movie.

ERIC
Get a real job like I did.

HADARA
I'll open my own business.
Nobody will ever fire me.

ERIC
Customers don't take old unknowns seriously.
Work the business side of life like an extrovert works a room.

HADARA
I never have trouble taking advice lately.
Why couldn't I listen when I was young?

ERIC
What did you really want to tell me?

HADARA
I forgive you and everyone else who needs forgiving, including me.
Now I can move up to take care of myself.
I was always afraid of being like my mom.
She couldn't take care of herself.
So she married a man who couldn't take care of a wife.

ERIC
The door is open.
Are you staying or moving on?
This is *my* house.
I paid the mortgage.

HADARA
That's why community property laws are a joke.

ERIC
You were homeless when we met.
I offered you a room and bath with kitchen privileges.
That's when I'm not eating in the kitchen.

HADARA
No job is *that* secure.
We *are* legally married.
I'll stay by choice.

FADE OUT/CURTAIN

END OF PLAY

Chapter Three

The Monologue

Adapting the Monologue to a One-Act Play
Adapt this monologue to a play or skit. Or re-write the monologue so that's it's suited to performance on the stage. Condense the monologue, if needed, to monologue length. You also can adapt this monologue to become a one-act play.

Name of Play, Skit or Monologue: What's My Core Identity?
This monologue is based on the three-act play above, *Coney Island*. How would you re-write it for the stage as a one-act monologue? It can be the same length as an average one-act play or shorter. If you condense it, select the significant highlights, events, and slices of life that are most powerful and memorable. Which words make the most impact on the audience?

Title: Core Identity[1]
(4,695 Words)

I still think of myself as a descendant of people who lived in ancient Greece and the old Greek islands and colonies. My paternal great grandmother born around 1834 in Bialystock, Poland, her daughter, Anna Katkowski, "The Cat"— born around 1854, my dad, one of nine children born (last in birth order) in 1894, my mom, from another land, born in 1904, whom dad married in 1926, and I born before World War Two, all were and are tired of being beaten up for looking Jewish. We've had it.

We're not tailoring our noses or tinting our hair any more. We look Middle Eastern, and we are tired of Middle Eastern people, whatever their religion getting beaten up for looking like they just stepped out of Babylon or Beirut.

My mother looked like the actress, Joan Collins in the movie "The Egyptian." I look like the sultry Italian actress, Anna Magnani. We are all Mediterranean-type women descended from Neolithic farmers of the grain belt born from women who lived centuries in Bialystock, Poland, and we are tired of getting our ears boxed for not always looking like Swedish milk maids in spite of some of us born with red hair, light eyes, fair complexions, and freckles. No matter how red our hair is or how green, blue, or hazel our eyes and light our skin, one look at our large, convex noses, and the shouts go up half in Yiddish, "Favus, Favus, she gotta longa nuz."

So who enriched my tapestry? How many tribes are in my temporary container? At the cellular level I have a cultural and biological component. Why did those two components lead me to spend seven years in an Arab Jewish intermarriage to see how the other side lives? Why did I spend seven years disguised as an Arab housewife in a Brooklyn Jewish neighborhood and then in California? And why did I finally marry an Anglo-Saxon?

My journey was in search of a core identity, but it led to something transcending even that—a link with all peoples through universal archetypes. What made us what we are besides the changing climate?

The earliest tales my mother wove, starting about the age of three, was about when the German mothers boxed her ears. It wasn't in Europe, but in Albany, New York. My mother was born in an old house in Albany, New York in 1904 to a woman from Bessarabia, Romania, (Ashkenazic Jews and Germans migrated from Poland, Ukraine, Latvia, Belarus, Germany, and Lithuania to Bessarabia in the 18th century), and a blond, silver-eyed man who looked almost exactly like Clark Gable, from Lodz, Poland. Dad's parents came from Bialystock, Poland in the late 19th century. If I'm supposed to be so pink-and-white Polish, how come I look like I just stepped out of Beirut?

I'm probably mixed. How mixed, only my DNA says, and my maternal DNA says I'm Northern European. So where's my core identity? Do I look on the paternal side and try to guess how many genes I share with Arabs compared to Northern Europeans? Is it important? No, it is not as much as in finding my core identity. I'm looking instead for the cultural components of my DNA rather than solely the biological components. I am what music heals me.

When my mother was two years old, her parents divorced and her mother gave her away to her father. He took her to Philadelphia. There, she was raised by a redheaded stepmother from Vienna, Austria and Odessa, Russia. As I grew up, my mother would tell me story after story of how she was beaten by hate crimes in the U.S. as a child. African-Americans beat her for having pink skin and silver eyes. Whites beat her for "looking Jewish" and having black and curly hair along with Mongolian features, supposedly inherited from the Khazars and the peoples of the Silk Road. And, gee, nobody beat her for looking like my mother. When she was ten in the fifth grade, she asked a fellow student, "Do I look Jewish?"

The student replied, "You got the map of Jerusalem printed on your face."

On and on, mom would talk to me, and each time, there was another tale of how she played with neighbor kids and their German mothers would box her ears and call her epithets with the word "Jew" in them. The stereotype is of anyone from a Mediterranean country or the Caucasus Mountains who happens to have the profile of King Sargon of Babylon as his mask portrayed thousands of years ago, or a Sicilian profile with fair skin, light eyes, and dark hair. So why is it important?

What's not symmetrical enough for you? Well neither was the profile of King Tut, or Pharaoh Ramses, (may his mummy rest in peace) and nobody puts his finger to his nose and curls it convexly, except in a 1971 "All in the Family" episode followed by familiar canned laughter.

My early childhood experienced World War II, in Brooklyn. We lived in a four-family house near Kings Highway. Between the ages of three and five, not only did mom tell me about the holocaust in Europe, because I was born in 1941, but she would rock me in her arms when I was three, sweating in anxiety, as she sang to me about the bombs that were coming to fall on New York pretty soon. There were lights out air raid drills, and always she told me the bombs were coming to fall, and they never did.

The sweating, the anxiety was there anyway, almost as if they had come. Then she'd tell me about how the Irish and German Americans used to beat her for looking Jewish in the neighborhoods. She grew up (aged 10 to 14) during World War One. The street we lived on had been mostly Jewish on one side and partly southern Italian on the other, and almost never the twain met or spoke to one another.

Mom was a battered wife. Not only did I experience the holocaust from her stories, but the battles inside my home. My father, age 47 when I was born, and my brother, 13 years older than I, beat mom. There were terrible fights. I hid in my room and drew cartoons of them fighting.

One day my father smashed my piano and violin and all my birthday toys because I kicked him out of the bed I slept in with my mother when he tried to enter the bed in the middle of the night to have sex with my mother.

I was nine, and I told him to get out. He slept in the room next door in twin beds with my older brother in the room. Men with men, women with women, throughout my parent's marriage. And he beat her. And she told me about how he beat her when she came home from the hospital with me a week old, and he punched her in the chest, and I fell from her arms into the snow. She had told him to hurry up and take the baby's picture because I was turning blue from the cold wind and snow.

My father always smashed things with hammers and axes. I was afraid someday he'd get me and kill me. Mom told me how much she worried, about everything, and most of all how awful it was to be Jewish and be beaten for looking Jewish. As I grew up, I began to look in the mirror and wonder whether I looked Jewish. I had a "Caspian Sea Nose."

My cousins told me "I looked very Semitic." So I began to make myself up to look like an ancient Egyptian, eye makeup, black wig or hair tint, and costume. As I grew into a teenager, I took up the Turkish Belly dance, the Egyptian cane dance, the Moroccan dance, and the Zamba-Mora, a mixture of Flamenco and Moorish. My ballet lessons started at the age of five. By the age of eleven I danced on point—(toe).

At nine I gave a performance in ballet, a solo on the stage at my elementary school. At seven I started violin lessons and at nine, piano lessons. Music became my life. At thirteen I added voice lessons. I went on to graduate from college as a creative writing major, fine art minor, with second minors in psychology and anthropology. I was into ethnomusicology and linguistics. My hobby was astronomy and illustration…writing poetry, novels.

Then, at 22, I took a train back from a vacation in Asbury Park, returning to New York. I was married at the time, to a non-Jew. It was 1964, and the movie, *Cleopatra* was all over town. I had tinted my hair black; made my eyes up to look Egyptian, and thought I looked like Liz Taylor when I gazed back at myself in the mirror. In August of 1964 I was married, two months pregnant, and then my self-image melted.

A man, who I call the neo-Nazi, told me not to cross between cars while the train was in motion until the train stopped in Elizabeth, New Jersey. He wasn't the conductor. He was a passenger with his wife. I couldn't understand why he would order me to "wait 'till the train stopped in Elizabeth." I told him I was pregnant and returning from the john, and needed to get back to my seat or my husband and mother riding in the next car would think I became ill in the bathroom. He ignored me.

So I passed in front of him to return to my seat. I didn't brush him or touch his luggage or anything. There was no conductor around, and normally the right procedure is when you walk from one train car to the next to use the bathroom, it's regular procedure to walk back to your seat in the next car by opening and closing the easily sliding doors.

There were no train rules broken, of course. Because I didn't defer and defied his command, by walking past him to reach the next car and return silently to my seat and husband, he grabbed my head in a vise-like grip. His knees squeezed together as he tried to crush my head between his knee and the wall of the train. He knew the tactic caused great pain in the skull. And he kicked me. The pain of my head being squeezed first between his large hands and then between his knees was unbearable.

Then he held me so I couldn't move and kicked me again, hard at the base of the spine while he yelled, "you dirty Jew." I went flying forward into the next car while his wife eyed my wedding ring as I faced her for a moment, and quietly smirked, "let her go, dear." She had the sweetest controlled voice as she looked up at me behind the fishnet veil of her pillbox hat. The two reminded me of the painting, "Gothic American." He was bald, black hair around the rim of his ears, staring black eyes, pale skin. She looked the same with curled brown hair and wrinkles above her thin lips. The words, "dirty Jew," rang in my head. I walked back to my seat two cars down and never said a word to my husband or mother.

My husband would have returned and started a fight. My mother had just gotten out of the hospital and was recuperating. For the next twenty years I never said a word...to anyone. My fear of being Jewish went inward and increased. When I wrote about my experience, some women accused me of being "a man-hater."

The next day I stopped trying to look like Elizabeth Taylor in *Cleopatra*. I bleached the black tint out of my brown hair and made it bright red. With the freckles and hazel green eyes, I announced to the mirror that I now looked Welsh. Funny, how nobody noticed my convex nose, I surmised, when my hair was medium ash blonde or Killarney russet.

A few times during my teenage years in Brooklyn, some Puerto Ricans asked me whether I were Scottish or Irish. One black man tried to strangle me without asking what I was first. He only asked where my money was. A white man asked me once where the synagogue was, but I remember seeing him on TV as one of the skinheads taken into custody.

He was teasing me. First he asked me whether I needed help crossing the street and called me old lady. When I told him my age as if to say, I'm not that old, he brought up the Jewish lady part, emphatically with fury and frustration.

I was over age 60-something then and turned around and told him this face is what Mediterranean people look like. At that point in a public street in a Mexican area of San Diego, I was disgusted and just tired of people asking me where I'm from and what I am. Every time I opened my mouth I was asked when I had come from New York. In one city, I walked into a seminar in Jewish history and heard that the professor had received death threats when he was appointed chairman of the Jewish Studies department that sponsored the free seminars at a university open to the public.

Most people who showed up were over age sixty and a few history students. So much for freedom of speech in a state university hall, it seems. The next lecture I went to was on quilting. The teacher never got any threats teaching crafts. All I went there for was to make a friend and find some place to belong. I still don't belong anywhere and have not yet made an attempt to make friends, although I want to. It became harder to find friends after age sixty-three, and I never learned to drive—too scared to take tests anymore.

It's more than forty years since I left Brooklyn. Why is it so important?

I seldom speak in public, but talk to my video camera frequently. Then I let the videos become available to individuals seeking information.

I've become a recluse to have some semblance of serenity. Better to be alone than to be 'pecked.' On the Internet people stop asking about my New York accent online. The silence of e-mail distracts them from even wanting to know. Interestingly enough, the man who beat me never bothered to ask first whether I was Jewish, Greek, or Armenian, or any other Eastern Mediterranean national or descended from, thereof, because we all look alike to him, but he singled out "Jew" and beat me for looking Jewish. I am an American with parents born in New York State.

What is Jewish supposed to look like, an Assyrian king of 3,500 years ago? Why do most Assyrian Christians look so much like me? With whom does my DNA cluster?

Why can't we all accept one another's diversity without asking, without making it so important to know what someone's core identity is in privacy. I'm not your egg donor, so why ask? Nearly each time I open my mouth someone asks me when I left New York. I've been out of New York since 1965.

The man on the train who beat me didn't ask my name or look to see whether I wore a cross or a star or anything else. For a moment I wanted to say, "I'm Maltese. This is the face of Malta, or Naples, or Istanbul, or Crete." Perhaps my 38 college units in anthropology would have come in handy at that moment. But I said nothing for decades after that event.

So scared was my mother of being Jewish that she first joined the Dutch reformed Protestant church in Brooklyn and took me there when I was nine. We landed in the Unitarian church for decades. I also went to many other churches in the neighborhood. At the Catholic Church, the nun once said to me, "I don't think you're Catholic. You look Jewish. What's your name?" I replied, "Angelica," because we lived near an Italian neighborhood, and I used to ask my Christian friends to donate their old rosaries to me because I collected them for those who needed them.

I learned my "hail Mary's" and pinned up all the rosaries in our basement where I lit a candle on Shabbat and prayed in Hebrew and in English, both the Catholic "hail Mary's" and the Jewish Sabbath blessing prayer every Friday night. I spoke to Jesus and anyone else listening and asked a lot of philosophical questions, and wrote a book of prayers when I was nearly twelve.

Then I started reading Tibetan Buddhism and all about reincarnation from other religions, including the Eastern religions. I saw religion as links on a chain knowing we all come from and go to the same place. A loving God would not have created people in the first place unless he, she, or it, the Creator or designer sent us to the same place equally and took us from that place to be born again and again. I wondered who wrote the Bible with all those inconsistencies and contradictions, but thought it was great to have all that control over people who really would do you wrong, and freedom to choose for all the people seeking for the highest right for the good of all.

I ended up marrying an Arab Sheik at 21. When I was pregnant, he beat the hell out of me. The marriage ended when I became a battered wife, and he took my two children to Syria where his mother and six brothers reared them after he divorced me and took away all the money in the bank, my furniture, and threw me out into the street after more than 6 years of marriage. At 33 I married a Protestant man, American, half German, half English. We are now married more than 30 years. I can't think of anyone who loves me, except my cat.

He used to beat me too, but far less than the Sheik, mostly more verbally, but twice a year physically, but now he's only verbally abusive and beats me only once a year if he can catch me when I run from him. He beats me only when we are moving from one house to another, and he's stressed. He has intermittent explosive disorder to some degree and explodes when he doesn't get his way, like when he wanted some old bookcases for fifty dollars, and I wanted something new.

I'm still married to him. He never reads what I write, and I write under different names. When he quiets down, he's back to his old withdrawn cold fish self just like daddy. We have not shared the same room for almost 30 years, his choice first, not mine, but now his snoring is loud enough to cause me insomnia. I've been celibate since 1976. He has no affection for me, but I don't have to pay rent. That's great as I don't have an income although I'd love an income.

When I think about it, I surmise on the MBTI "! I m an INFP. A wife isn t supposed to complain about her cold-fish husband according to etiquette, but I m a woman who can t take care of herself married to a man who can t take care of a wife. He s a commanding, bullying, whining and volcanic ISFJ with low serotonin levels, high narcissism and worry about self image. I'm shy, frightened, old, and spent, but I like the free rent, the backyard, and my doggies who do show me affection by wagging their tails when I give them their food and a hug.

My husbands became abusive dads to me, just like my own dad, but since my present husband abuses me far less than the first husband did, I'll stay as long as there's money to pay the taxes on the house and keep food in the fridge.

I married my first husband at 21, the Sheik because I thought in a previous life, I had come from Egypt or Syria, but digging deeper, I found at that at 13 I was secretly in love with a Syrian Jewish boy in my class because he was rich, lived in a private house on Ocean Parkway, and was handsome.

A clique of Syrian Jewish girls said I could join their 8th grade sorority if I took all my clothes off in front of them and let their 6-year old brother feel me up. Wanting so bad to join their clique, I went into the closet and took off all my clothes. The girls grabbed my clothes, tossed them over my head, playing monkey in the middle, and humiliated me.

Then they pushed me out of their house and into the gutter with me barely missing the path of an oncoming car by inches. I was totally intimidated and humiliated. Thereafter, I never had a friend for years.

Later, I tried making friends with a Jewish girl. She was rich, an Ashkenazi, and became my best friend. But she betrayed me like the others. When I confided in her, making her like a sister, that my mom was arrested for shoplifting and I was so shocked, she turned around and made up a lie that I had stolen her empty purse. Her mother called my brother and screamed about my mother being a shoplifter. She never knew my mother. I didn't take her purse and never would have thought such thoughts.

All I wanted to be is accepted by the rich, or those richer than I was. Her father practiced law. Mine was a janitor and 8th-grade dropout, born in 1894 in New York. She kept asking me to return the purse. I kept asking why she'd make up such as story and then tell her mother about my mother, or why her mother would call my older brother and rub his nose in the dirt that my mother was arrested for shoplifting, when I had told her daughter this in confidence as my best friend.

Needless to say, I have no friends today, no living relatives beyond my distant children that I know of, and a husband who puts me down verbally, teases me, and sometimes batters me. People seem to have betrayed me a lot. And yet, I still hope someday I'll find a friend. I'm no longer sociophobic. Nor do I walk through life totally alone any more. I can choose joining associations or meditating in isolation, usually home-based. I spend many days reading and writing or walking through the zoo.

One freedom I cherish. It's to belong to several religions at one time and to attend all the churches, synagogues, or other houses of worship that I want—usually the Unitarian. I go to Christian churches on Christian holidays and to Jewish synagogues on Jewish holidays.

I want my freedom to choose any religion anytime and to attend any celebration of life. I cherish this freedom because I believe God is love and that we all come from and go to the same place. No creator creates any intelligent being unequal to any other intelligent being on any universe. And our companion pets come with us into eternity and give us comfort.

For a decade I was housebound with agoraphobia and panic between age 23 and 33. It burned itself out without any treatment, as I was penniless. Today, I have two computers, a paid-off home, and it's all his. I'm still too scared to tell anyone I'm Jewish, except other Jews. I belong to the Unitarian church, and I still celebrate, alone, the Jewish holidays.

My two children are devout Muslims, still trying to convert me to Islam and talking about Jews at the same time, warning me not to tell their friends that I'm Jewish. I smile to their face. I'm forbidden to tell my grandchildren my religion. What religion? I'm one with the universe because we all come from and go back to the exact same place. I'll read the book or Bible of any religion and contemplate all the good points.

Why am I scared to be Jewish? The Skinheads and Neo Nazis are all over this town. I am respected in the Unitarian church. I give donations to the Jewish organizations. Secretly, I sneak off to "Chabad" and dance with the "Hassids," clapping my hands in joy. On Christmas I'm in the Unitarian church listening to the fine carols and playing them on my organ in a celebration of life. And I still belly dance to Middle Eastern music when I'm alone at home. I love all peoples and cherish their music as a divine gift to humankind. In soothing music from all cultures I find the harmony and serenity of healing.

My mother always said that someday there's going to be another holocaust right here in America and they'll get me if I tell anyone I'm Jewish. I really don't know when or if that might happen. I pray not. I cherish the freedom of religion and the separation of church and state.

Taking away one's freedom of worship is akin to being told you have the wrong country's nose and that a surgeon must take off what identifies you. It's like being told that thousands of years ago an ancestor came from a certain place and that has to be corrected. A plastic surgeon once said he'd take the hump off my nose, but what's the point? I don't need symmetry to feel beautiful on the outside or inside. I need the experience of joyful song. I hope no more mayhem will happen, hope so much that I pray tensely with my eyelids squeezed shut.

The only thing I can do about it is to try to make the world a kinder and gentler place, being the idealist that I am as I do my housewifely crafts and write a novel a year to keep active. I go to the Unitarian church and hold my head up high, and I go to the synagogue and hold my head up high, and I don't want anybody calling me ethnic names or hating me because my great-great grandparents practiced a particular religion in a country I've never seen.

My favorite author is Ray Bradbury. We all see things, not the way they are, but the way we are. A hate crime doesn't have to play on stage where observers can distance themselves. Fear doesn't have to take top billing publicly; it can be internal.

When will it be okay anywhere in the world to follow your spiritual meditations privately and not be chastised publicly for your symmetry or hue?

How are we all doing with visual shorthand? I have not "gotten a life." Instead, I've learned to forgive others and myself. Why would a nice, Jewish girl from Coney Island marry an Arab Sheik *and live disguised as an Arab housewife in a Jewish section of Brooklyn for nearly seven years?* Maybe because we all come from and go to the same place or maybe because in a former life I was both, maybe I'm looking for something beyond a core identity, or maybe I just want a connection to everyone else in the world, but on a higher plane that reaches beyond territory and tribe to universal archetypes.

After all, you get to the universal only through the concrete details with which we all identify across cultures. Everyone on the planet is connected by a common ancestor. I'm connected to the three fellows who lived somewhere in the Middle East 7,800 years ago, the woman who lived in Europe 20,000 years ago, and the rest who left the Fertile Crescent, Central Asia, Africa, or India between 60,000 and 30,000 years ago for better campgrounds. They are all connected to me by my DNA and love of art, music, and writing.

*   *   *

Core Identity [2]
Another Version for Monologue to One-Act Play
Adapt This Monologue Version for Your One-Act Play
Add More Characters from the Three-Act Play
Word Count: 2,991

"Belle Wietzmann, born in Lodz, Poland in 1861, a distant relative of Chaim Weitzmann, President of Israel," the genealogist revealed with pride to my aunt. Belle Weitzmann is my mother's dad's mother's maiden name. Belle married Israel Tucker, whose son, born in 1880, Chaim Muni Tucker, had Anglicized his name to Herman Tucker.

My mom, afraid of being rejected or beaten by telling non-Jews she was Jewish, led two lives in our home, Unitarian with me and Jewish from Lodz, Poland circa 1890 with my brother and dad.

It's all because the housing laws years ago didn't allow Jews to buy housing in certain parts of the country that my family coveted, particularly the palm latitudes. Housing laws changed after 1950, but my core identity didn't change with the new housing laws.

According to the article, "Flaw in the Jewel: Housing Discrimination Against Jews in La Jolla, CA,"—American Jewish History 84:3 (1996) 189-219, when Dr. Jonas Salk, the first Jew to move to La Jolla, CA moved next door to a non-Jew, that person put his/her house on the market. What's my core identity? What do I have to be to buy a house in the Garden of Eden—beachside, California? So we all turned Protestant and tinted our medium brown hair medium ash blonde.

The family's green eyes fitted in perfectly with our new English names. Why did we have to do this to buy a house? Even my DNA says I'm not 'Jewish'—but Lithuanian. So who am I? My great, great grandfather was a rabbi. I'm the only Jewish member of my family left, and I've always worshipped alone.

What I miss most is belonging to a family, but there's no one left. So I have to embrace all the religions the surviving younger generation has embraced. No one gets left out, but no one has included me. I'm pushing 70, and I don't have a family who ever visits.

My paternal great grandmother born around 1834 in Bialystock, Poland, her daughter, Anna Kutkowski, "The Cat"—born around 1854, my dad, one of nine children born (last in birth order) in 1894, my mom, from another land, born in 1904, whom dad married in 1926, and I born before World War Two, all were and are tired of being beaten up for looking Jewish. We've had it.

We're not tailoring our noses or tinting our hair any more. We look Middle Eastern, and we are tired of Middle Eastern people, whatever their religion getting beaten up for looking like they just stepped out of Babylon or Beirut.

My mother looked like the actress, Joan Collins in the movie "The Egyptian." I look like the sultry Italian actress, Anna Magnani. We are all Mediterranean-type women descended from Neolithic farmers of the grain belt born from women who lived centuries in Bialystock, Poland, and we are tired of getting our ears boxed for not always looking like Swedish milk maids in spite of some of us born with red hair, light eyes, fair complexions, and freckles. No matter how red our hair is or how green, blue, or hazel our eyes and light our skin, one look at our large, convex noses, and the shouts go up half in Yiddish, "Favus, Favus, she gotta longa nuz."

So who enriched my tapestry? How many tribes are in my temporary container? My journey was in search of a core identity, but it led to something transcending even that—a link with all peoples through universal archetypes. What made us what we are besides the changing climate?

The earliest tales my mother wove, starting about the age of three, was about when the German mothers boxed her ears. It wasn't in Europe, but in Albany, New York. My mother was born in an old house in Albany, New York in 1904 to a woman from Bessarabia, Romania, (Ashkenazic Jews and Germans migrated from Poland, Ukraine, Latvia, Belarus, Germany, and Lithuania to Bessarabia in the 18th century), and a blond, silver-eyed man who looked almost exactly like Clark Gable, from Lodz, Poland. Dad's parents came from Bialystock, Poland in the late 19th century. If I'm supposed to be so pink-and-white Polish, how come I look like I just stepped out of Beirut?

How I am mixed, only my DNA says, and my maternal DNA says I'm Northern European. It's not important how I'm mixed, only that I'm not mixed up.

When my mother was two years old, her parents divorced and her mother gave her away to her father. He took her to Philadelphia. There, she was raised by a redheaded stepmother from Vienna, Austria and Odessa, Russia. As I grew up, my mother would tell me story after story of how she was beaten by hate crimes in the U.S. as a child. African-Americans beat her for having pink skin and silver eyes.

Whites beat her for "looking Jewish" and having black and curly hair along with Mongolian features, supposedly inherited from the Khazars and the peoples of the Silk Road. And, gee, nobody beat her for looking like my mother. When she was ten in the fifth grade, she asked a fellow student, "Do I look Jewish?"

The student replied, "You got the map of Jerusalem printed on your face."

On and on, mom would talk to me, and each time, there was another tale of how she played with neighbor kids and their German mothers would box her ears and call her epithets with the word "Jew" in them. The stereotype is of anyone from a Mediterranean country or the Caucasus Mountains who happens to have the profile of King Sargon of Babylon as his mask portrayed thousands of years ago, or a Sicilian profile with fair skin, light eyes, and dark hair. So why is it important?

What's not symmetrical enough for you? Well neither was the profile of King Tut, or Pharaoh Ramses, (may his mummy rest in peace) and nobody puts his finger to his nose and curls it convexly, except in a 1971 "All in the Family" episode followed by familiar canned laughter.

My early childhood experienced World War II, in Brooklyn. We lived in a four-family house near Kings Highway. Between the ages of three and five, not only did mom tell me about the holocaust in Europe, because I was born in 1941, but she would rock me in her arms when I was three, sweating in anxiety, as she sang to me about the bombs that were coming to fall on New York pretty soon.

There were lights out air raid drills, and always she told me the bombs were coming to fall, and they never did.

The sweating, the anxiety was there anyway, almost as if they had come. Then she'd tell me about how the Irish and German Americans used to beat her for looking Jewish in the neighborhoods. She grew up (aged 10 to 14) during World War One. The street we lived on had been mostly Jewish on one side and partly southern Italian on the other, and almost never the twain met or spoke to one another.

Mom was a battered wife. Not only did I experience the holocaust from her stories, but the battles inside my home. My father, age 47 when I was born, and my brother, 13 years older than I, beat mom. There were terrible fights. I hid in my room and drew cartoons of them fighting.

One day my father smashed my piano and violin and all my birthday toys because I kicked him out of the bed I slept in with my mother when he tried to enter the bed in the middle of the night to have sex with my mother.

I was nine, and I told him to get out. He slept in the room next door in twin beds with my older brother in the room. The rule stood firm: men with men, women with women—throughout my parent's marriage. And dad beat mom. She told me about how he beat her when she came home from the hospital with me a week old, and he punched her in the chest, and I fell from her arms into the snow. She had told him to hurry up and take the baby's picture because I was turning blue from the cold wind and snow.

My father always smashed things with hammers and axes. I was afraid someday he'd get me and kill me. Mom told me how much she worried, about everything, and most of all how awful it was to be Jewish and be beaten for looking Jewish. As I grew up, I began to look in the mirror and wonder whether I looked Jewish. I had a "Caspian Sea Nose."

My cousins told me "I looked very Semitic." So I began to make myself up to look like an ancient Egyptian, eye makeup, black wig or hair tint, and costume. As I grew into a teenager, I took up the Turkish Belly dance, the Egyptian cane dance, the Moroccan dance, and the Zamba-Mora, a mixture of Flamenco and Moorish. My ballet lessons started at the age of five. By the age of eleven I danced on point—(toe).

At nine I gave a performance in ballet, a solo on the stage at my elementary school. At seven I started violin lessons and at nine, piano lessons. Music became my life. At thirteen I added voice lessons. I went on to graduate from college as a creative writing major, fine art minor, with second minors in psychology and anthropology. I was into ethnomusicology and linguistics. My hobby was astronomy and illustration…writing poetry, novels.

Then, at 22, I took a train back from a vacation in Asbury Park, returning to New York. I was married at the time, to a non-Jew. It was 1964, and the movie, *Cleopatra* was all over town. I had tinted my hair black; made my eyes up to look Egyptian, and thought I looked like Liz Taylor when I gazed back at myself in the mirror. In August of 1964 I was married, two months pregnant, and then my self-image melted.

A man, who I call the neo-Nazi, told me not to cross between cars while the train was in motion until the train stopped in Elizabeth, New Jersey. He wasn't the conductor. He was a passenger with his wife. I couldn't understand why he would order me to "wait 'till the train stopped in Elizabeth." I told him I was pregnant and returning from the john, and needed to get back to my seat or my husband and mother riding in the next car would think I became ill in the bathroom. He ignored me.

So I passed in front of him to return to my seat. I didn't brush him or touch his luggage or anything. There was no conductor around, and normally the right procedure is when you walk from one train car to the next to use the bathroom, it's regular procedure to walk back to your seat in the next car by opening and closing the easily sliding doors.

There were no train rules broken, of course. Because I didn't defer and defied his command, by walking past him to reach the next car and return silently to my seat and husband, he grabbed my head in a vise-like grip with his hand and knee, squeezed, trying to crush my head between his knee and the wall of the train causing me great pain in the skull, and beat the hell out of me by squeezing my head. The pain of my head being squeezed first between his large hands and then between his knees was unbearable.

Then he held me so I couldn't move and kicked me hard at the base of the spine while he yelled, "you dirty Jew." I went flying forward into the next car while his wife eyed my wedding ring as I faced her for a moment, and quietly smirked, "let her go, dear."

She had the sweetest controlled voice as she looked up at me behind the fish-net veil of her pillbox hat. The two reminded me of the painting, "Gothic American." He was bald, black hair around the rim of his ears, staring black eyes, pale skin. She looked the same with curled brown hair and wrinkles above her thin lips. The words, "dirty Jew," rang in my head. I walked back to my seat two cars down and never said a word to my husband or mother.

My husband would have returned and started a fight. My mother had just gotten out of the hospital and was recuperating. For the next twenty years I never said a word...to anyone. My fear of being Jewish went inward and increased. When I wrote about my experience, some women accused me of being "a man-hater."

The next day I stopped trying to look like Elizabeth Taylor in *Cleopatra*. I bleached the black tint out of my brown hair and made it bright red. With the freckles and hazel green eyes, I announced to the mirror that I now looked Welsh. Funny, how nobody noticed my convex nose, I surmised, when my hair was medium ash blonde or Killarney russet.

A few times during my teenage years in Brooklyn, some Puerto Ricans asked me whether I were Scottish or Irish. One black man tried to strangle me without asking what I was first. He only asked where my money was. A white man asked me once where the synagogue was, but I remember seeing him on TV as one of the skinheads taken into custody.

He was teasing me. First he asked me whether I needed help crossing the street and called me old lady. When I told him my age as if to say, I'm not that old, he brought up the Jewish lady part, emphatically with fury and frustration.

I was over age 60-something then and turned around and told him this face is what Mediterranean people look like. At that point in a public street in a Mexican area of San Diego, I was disgusted and just tired of people asking me where I'm from and what I am. Every time I opened my mouth I was asked when I had come from New York. In one city, I walked into a seminar in Jewish history and heard that the professor had received death threats when he was appointed chairman of the Jewish Studies department that sponsored the free seminars at a university open to the public.

Most people who showed up were over age sixty and a few history students. So much for freedom of speech in a state university hall, it seems. The next lecture I went to was on quilting. The teacher never got any threats teaching crafts. All I went there for was to make a friend and find some place to belong. I still don't belong anywhere and have not yet made an attempt to make friends, although I want to. It became harder to find friends after age sixty-three, and I never learned to drive—too scared to take tests anymore.

It's more than forty years since I left Brooklyn. Why is it so important?

I seldom speak in public, but talk to my video camera frequently. Then I let the videos become available to individuals seeking information.

I've become a recluse to have some semblance of serenity. Better to be alone than to be 'pecked.' On the Internet people stop asking about my New York accent online.

What is Jewish supposed to look like, an Assyrian king of 3,500 years ago? Why do most Assyrian Christians look so much like me? With whom does my DNA cluster? Why can't we all accept one another's diversity without asking, without making it so important to know what someone's core identity is in privacy. I'm not your egg donor, so why ask? Nearly each time I open my mouth someone asks me when I left New York. I've been out of New York since 1965.

The man on the train who beat me didn't ask my name or look to see whether I wore a cross or a star or anything else. For a moment I wanted to say, "I'm Maltese. This is the face of Malta, or Naples, or Istanbul, or Crete." Perhaps my 38 college units in anthropology would have come in handy at that moment. But I said nothing for decades after that event.

So scared was my mother of being Jewish that she first joined the Dutch reformed Protestant church in Brooklyn and took me there when I was nine. We landed in the Unitarian church for decades. I also went to many other churches in the neighborhood. At the Catholic Church, the nun once said to me, "I don't think you're Catholic. You look Jewish. What's your name?" I replied, "Angelica," because we lived near an Italian neighborhood, and I used to ask my Christian friends to donate their old rosaries to me because I collected them for those who needed them.

I saw religion as links on a chain knowing we all come from and go to the same place. A loving God would not have created people in the first place unless he, she, or it, the Creator or designer sent us to the original source of life equally and took us from that original source of life to be born again and again.

I wondered how many different people wrote the Bible over so many years with all those Bible codes, predictions, inconsistencies, and contradictions, but thought it was great to have all that control over people who really would do you wrong. The Almighty's greatest gift to us is the freedom to choose for all the people seeking the highest right for the good of everyone in every universe where life exists.

Chapter Four

Writing for Puppet Theatre

Adapting Scriptwriting for Animation to Puppet Theater for Children

Re-write this animation script as a stage play for children using the concept of animal puppets in costume. It's 24 pages in length and runs about 6,367 words. You can write this for puppets or for children in costume or puppets children can make.

Puppet movements on a puppet stage substitute for camera angles or camera shots. Write in the direction choosing either puppet actions or live children dressed in animal costumes. With puppets you can simulate the flight of birds across a puppet stage.

This makes it easier to adapt as a puppet theater script. This exercise gives you practice and experience in writing for puppet theater, children's theater, and animation scriptwriting. Camera direction such as "fade in" can be substituted for lighting variations and sounds on a puppet stage.

*   *   *

THE AMAZON HATCHLINGS

In

"PICKLES, THE PARROT"

A 12-Minute Pilot Script for a New Animation Series

(12 minutes)

THE AMAZON HATCHLINGS

in

PICKLES, THE PARROT

By

Anne Hart

FADE IN:

ON A CLOSE SHOT OF A LARGE RAINBOW TOUCAN

rapidly chewing down an Amazon Parrotberry tree. CAMERA WIDENS to reveal a whole flock of toucans stripping the tree of all berries and leaves. The tree is soon chewed down to a nub.

CLOSER ON PICKLES, THE AMAZON YELLOW NAPE PARROT, as he sticks his head out of a window putting a steaming Parrotberry pie on his window sill to cool.

PICKLES

Those toucans are eating all

our Parrotberry trees.

CAMERA WIDENS to reveal the parrot family: Old Macaw, Parette, Hatchling, a tiny ball of fluff with a beak, Nestling, and Fledgling inside the highrise bamboo birdcage house building scarecrows to chase the toucans away from the parrotberry tree. OLD MACAW is building a bird cage in the middle of the floor instead of a scarecrow.

CLOSER ON OLD MACAW

MACAW

Your scarecrow won't scare 'em

for long. But I'm building them a

home of their own.

PICKLES

When there aren't any more

Parrotberries left, the toucans

will move to another spot.

CLOSER ON PICKLES

PICKLES takes a magical salt shaker out of his pocket and
seasons a bowl of fruit from the table.

PICKLES

This will attract the toucans

away from the Parrotberry tree.

When they smell these salts,

they'll stop eating Parrotberries.

Pickles stuffs fruit into his pockets and into the pockets
of all the Amazon Babies, including Hatchling, also putting
seasoned plums under Hatchling's bonnet.

FLEDGLING

You mean our last Parrotberry tree.

PICKLES

I'll sprinkle my toucan bait

powder on all this fruit.

PICKLES grabs a cord he's attached to the bird cage and gives
it a pull. SFX: OUTBOARD MOTOR SPUTTER

WIDER ANGLE

as the birdcage starts to glide across the floor. PICKLES
points ahead. All the AMAZON HATCHLINGS hop aboard through the open
door of the cage and hold onto one another as they sit
on the bird cage swing and perches.

PICKLES

That tree over there looks swell.

As they move out of shot we cut to:

THE TREETOPS OF A LARGE GROVE OF PARROTBERRY TREES

The HATCHLINGS gain into shot in an animated bird cage
helicopter/motorboat combo. They take fruit and nuts
out of their pockets and bait the birdcage to attract
the toucans. Fledgling leans over the edge, looks
down at the toucans on the Parrotberry tree branches.

FLEDGLING

Amazonadoodle! I hope the toucans

find the fruit in their new home

tastes better than our Parrotberry

branches.

CLOSER ON FLEDGLING AND PICKLES

FLEDGLING screeches as the chewed branch gives way.

PICKLES

Oh, no! There's nothing to

hang the cage on up here. Help.

WIDE ON CAGE

as cage begins to crash through the hollow, eaten out
tree. The tree falls over, entirely stripped of branches
and berries. In mid-air PICKLES pulls a balloon out of
his pocket and, huffing and puffing, inflates it. He
attaches the balloon to the top of the birdcage and it
floats above the next treetop.

CLOSE ON GRANDPA MACAW IN CAGE

GRANDPA MACAW

Look! That tree still has some

Parrotberries left on it.

WIDE ON CAGE

as it floats to the next treetop and settles on a branch.
HATCHLING holds out a plum and a toucan flies over and takes it
out of the HATCHLING's hand.

THREE-SHOT PICKLES, GRANDPA MACAW, AND HATCHLING

GRANDPA MACAW

They are taking the fruit.

PICKLES

Now, if only they'll all fly

into the nice birdcage.

CLOSE ON HATCHLING

HATCHLING burbles, flaps his tiny wings and climbs out on the tree branch to pet the nice toucan as the bird gobbles up the plum.

> NESTLING
>
> No, Hatchling, don't follow
>
> that toucan.

The toucan looks up at Hatchliing with a mischievous twinkle in its blue eye as it flies under Hatchling. Hatchling wraps his baby wings around the toucan's outstretched neck as it takes off into a rainbow with Hatchling holding on, riding the toucan.

> GRANDPA MACAW
>
> Come back, Hatchling!

ANGLE ON PICKLES, GRANDPA MACAW AND NESTLING

> PICKLES
>
> We must find out where the
>
> toucans are coming from.

> GRANDPA MACAW
>
> They're probably taking
>
> Hatchling to toucan's cove.

> NESTLING
>
> With all that fruit I
>
> stuffed in Hatchling's knapsack,

it will attract every

bird in the Amazon.

ANGLE ON SILLY AND JESTER

SILLY takes a little yellow wormlike noodle out of a
container, and grimaces.

JESTER

Yeuk! What kind of birds

would want to eat those?

JESTER holds a similar container. He takes a noodle
wormlike thing out of his container.

SILLY

These vegetarian worms

are great for toucans.

They only eat veggies,

just like parrots.

SILLY pops it into his mouth, swallows it, and licks
his lips. JESTER frowns.

WIDER ANGLE

JESTER

Yeuck! Vanity swallowed

a worm or a baby snake.

SILLY

Toucans don't eat real

worms! These are fried fruitnoodles.

He takes another handful, stuffs them into his mouth.
SILLY looks at his container.

JESTER

No, they're my fish-bait worms.

These are fried fruitnoodles!

CLOSE ON SILLY

as he does an abrupt take, his cheeks stuffed. SILLY looks
down into his container. A little yellow baby snake pokes
its head up, looks and him and gurgles, making an evil,
angry face. SILLY looks into camera, swallows hard, then
breaks out into loud laughter.

SILLY

Well, if it's good enough

for the toucans, it's okay

with me.

ANGLE ON FLEDGLING AND DROOPY

as they walk into shot. FLEDGLING wears a bird-house hat with all types of
bird lures on it. DROOPY wears a vest with pockets from which hang transpar-
ent bags of seeds. They both wear
artificial wings. DROOPY holds a long pole with a radar screen on the handle
and artificial wings and a guided missile lure on the end of the pole that detects
birds before they reach a Parrotberry tree. DROOPY puts on a toucan's beak
mask.

DROOPY

This is my toucan-detecting missile.

It's a radar detector that shows me

when strange birds are

approaching our Parrotberry trees.

All you have to do is turn it on

and it automatically finds those toucans.

FLEDGLING

Why don't you try it out?

FLEDGLING hands the pole to DROOPY who presses a button on
the radar controller and the guided missile fires up,
shooting away with a LOUD ROCKET ENGINE SOUND, dragging
out the line. DROOPY jumps back as the bird detecting
missile spirals around DROOPY'S wings.
The missile springs a net and ties DROOPY into a
bird's nest of twigs and twine.

FLEDGLING

Amazoneroops! My device thought

you were a toucan. Better take

off that toucan bannana beak.

Now we can see DROOPY'S eyes blink in a perplexed way and his feathers stand
on end like a ruffled bird.

DISSOLVE TO:

INT. PAPA YELLOW NAPE'S HOUSE-SHORT TIME LATER

Carrying a large bird net, PAPA YELLOW NAPE ENTERS SHOT from the
stairway.

PAPA YELLOW NAPE

Everybody knows eagles taste awful.

WIDER ON EAGLE IN SKYEAGLE soars again until the bird becomes a black dot on top of the mountain's peak.

CLOSER ON EAGLE, FLEDGLING,

                              EAGLE

                    He thinks that you'd send

                    eagles and hawks to chase

                    the toucans away from your

                    parrotberries.

                              FLEDGLING

                    So if we get your eaglets

                    back for you, then will you promise

                    never to take our parrotlings?

ANGLE ON EAGLE

                              EAGLE

                    Sure. I don't like cream of

                    hookbill soup anyway. My

                    eaglets would much rather

                    have leftover chicken.

WIDER ON PICKLES, GRANDPA MACAW, EAGLE

PICKLES

Let's sneak into Hawk's castle.

EAGLE

If I snatch his pet iguana in my claws,

as I fly, Hawk will follow me.

GRANDPA MACAW

Then we can return the eaglets

to you.

DISSOLVE

EXT.-NEAR THE EDGE OF THE AMAZON-THE NEXT MORNING

HATCHLING sits in the shade of a hollowed tree, playing with his
magical bracelet. Parette looks overhead to see hundreds of
new toucans swarming through the groves of parrrotberry trees.

WIDER ON PICKLES AND EAGLE

PICKLES is putting together a type of harness on the EAGLE'S back.
The harness has three seats on it. PICKLES, PAPA YELLOW NAPE, and
FLEDGLING hop on board the EAGLE'S back and put on goggles. The eagle
soars skyward as PARETTE and HATCHLING wave to the three. The EAGLE
grows smaller and finally disappears into the sky toward Bald Eagle Mountain
and the EAGLE'S nest.

CUT TO:

EXT. EAGLE'S NEST ON TOP OF BALD EAGLE MOUNTAIN-DAY

There is sunshine, blue sky with clouds, and lots of grass
and greenery. It is pleasant and warm. We see the EAGLE'S nest
with hatched, empty cracked eggshells strewn around the
outside of the nest. The EAGLE paces to and fro awkwardly

with her wings spread.

PICKLES, PAPA YELLOW NAPE, AND FLEDGLING strut around following in back of the EAGLE, pacing, copying the same movements as the EAGLE.

CUT TO:

HAWK'S PET IGUANA PICKS UP THE EAGLETS, ONE BY ONE, AND DROPS THEM INTO A BASKET TO HAWK, WAITING BELOW.
CUT TO:
ANGLE ON PICKLES as he

peers over the ledge of the enormously steep cliff,
a yawning ravine.

> PICKLES
>
> There's a ledge down there to land on.

FLEDGLING peers over.

> FLEDGLING
>
> Look! There's a yawning ravine.

FLEDGLING points. Below is a grey stone rock that looks like a huge open yawning mouth. It's an entrance to a cave.

CLOSE ON PICKLES, FLEDGLING, AND EAGLE

PICKLES takes a rope out of his back pack and ties it to a rock
near the EAGLE'S nest. The EAGLE takes it's big nest in its beak
and moves it to PICKLES. FLEDGLING helps PICKLES tie the rope onto a
loop in the nest.

FLEDGLING

I'll stay up here with Eagle

and build a trap in case Hawk

comes back to the scene of the crime.

PICKLES

If we're not back by sundown, Eagle,

come and parrot us to safety.

EAGLE nods his head up and down agreeably.

FLEDGLING gently lowers the basket holding PAPA YELLOW NAPE and PICKLES as EAGLE helps by holding the rope in its beak. EAGLE and FLEDG-LING peer over the ledge of the vertical cliff as FLEDGLING ties the rope to the rock even more securely.

DISSOLVE TO:

INT. INSIDE DARKISH CAVE.

WIDER ON ENORMOUS CAVE.

STALAGTITES AND STALAGMITES, hang like limestone needles from the cave. (It looks like the interior of Carlsbad Caverns). It is dark, but with an eerie red light coming from an opening in the
distance ahead. This is Hawk's summer palace.

WIDE ON PAPA YELLOW NAPE, AND PICKLES

as they enter a brightly lighted room. There is a huge swimming pool surrounded by classical Roman and Greek statues. The pool
is rimmed by turquoise, blue and white mosaic tile. There are
tall, gothic windows. The white marble statues circle the large, kidney-shaped pool. The walls are tiled in the blue, white and turquoise fleur-de-lis mosaic tile. The pool has an open skylight
roof—an atrium where the sun's rays shine down into the pool

to show hazy beams of light.

PAPA YELLOW NAPE and PICKLES tiptoe around the pool.

CLOSER ON PICKLES AND PAPA YELLOW NAPE

> PICKLES
>
> Look how real those marble statues look.

ANGLE ON ONE "GREEK" STATUE
One tear drop begins to trickle down the cheek on one male marble
statue standing beside the pool. SFX: The tears plink into the pool.

> PAPA YELLOWNAPE
>
> Slithering sparrows!
>
> That statue's crying real tears.

PICKLES sidles up to the statue and looks deeply into its eyes.

CLOSE ON EYES OF STATUE
The eyes give PICKLES a pleading look for help.

> PICKLES
>
> You're right. These aren't statues.
>
> Hawk's turned these people to
>
> marble to line his swimming pool.

ANGLE ON STATUE'S ARM

as it points to a bend in the cavern ahead.

WIDER ON PICKLES AND PAPA YELLOW NAPE

PAPA YELLOW NAPE

That statue's pointing to the light

ahead.

The two scramble in the direction the statue is pointing.
They stumble upon a huge aviary filled with the eaglets
and other very rare birds, including blue macaws, green parrots, red cardinals, etc.
The aviary is perched on a ledge high on the
stalagmites and under the stalagtites. Brainy climbs up on the
ledge and unlocks the birdcage door.

PICKLES

Okay eaglets and other birds.

You're free now, and big enough to fly away home.

All the BIRDS make an exit from the huge cage, except for the
eaglets. They look up sadly and vulnerable at PICKLES.

PAPA YELLOWNAPE

Those eaglets are babies. They're too

young to fly. Let's stuff them in

our pockets.

PICKLES puts out his wing and the eaglets crawl onto the wing and into his
pockets. The two eaglets, Vali and Vanda, sit on top of Pickles' wings. He gives
one to PAPA.

EAGLET VALI

I'm Vali.

EAGLET VANDA

And I'm Vanda.

VALI AND VANDA

(speaking together)

We wander.

The eaglet nestlings are cute and irresistable little cottony puffballs.

VALI

Would you happen to have a

chili dog on you?

ANGLE ON PAPA YELLOW NAPE

PAPA

Don't worry. We'll return you

to your mother.

WIDER ON HAWK'S IGUANA, SCREECHER

hiding on the ledge, posed to leap.
SCREECHER is perched on a ledge above the empty aviary. He snarls angrily, baring his teeth, and leaps for the eaglets on PAPA YELLOW NAPE'S wings. PAPA YELLOW NAPES flaps his wings and a strong wind blows them into his claws in time to save the eaglet from SCREECHER'S grasp.

VANDA

Help! That iguana's going to have

us all for dinner.

IGUANA SCREECHER snarls viciously, snaps and screeches.

Stars appear and a beam swirls bright light as HAWK appears in his royal evil magician's robes.

ANGLE ON HAWK, PAPA YELLOW NAPE, PICKLES.

HAWK shoves PAPA YELLOW NAPE and PICKLES back into the aviary. He slams the door of the bird cage as the two eaglets peer out of each of PAPA YEL-LOW NAPE'S pockets.

HAWK

(laughing menacingly and rubbing his wings)

Guard them well, Screecher.

SCREECHER circles and paces around the cage like a dragon.

CLOSER on the SHADOW of SCREECHER, which looms much larger as a black silhouette of dragon doom on the walls of the cave. HAWK pulls a torch off the wall and lights it with a candle on a table. He places the lighted torch back in its slot on the cave wall. An eerie light flickers as SCREECHER paces back and forth around
the bird cage, guarding the captured parrots and eaglets.

DISSOLVE TO:

HAWK'S KITCHEN

HAWK is rapidly slicing carrots and throwing them into a pot of boiling water.

HAWK

Oh, there's nothing more delicious

than a parrot casserole over a crusty

eaglet pie. For dessert I'll have

stuffed mushrooms and cloves

on sizzling parrot steak.

ANGLE ON SCREECHER

As the iguana watches HAWK dice his veggies.

WIDER ON HAWK AND SCREECHER

HAWK looks up at SCREECHER.

> HAWK
>
> I thought you're supposed to be watching
> that bird cage.

> SCREECHER
>
> (looks down sheepishly)

> HAWK
>
> Naughty iguana. We'll you can stay here
> for now and help me prepare the pie
> crust.

> SCREECHER
>
> (delighted growl)

CLOSER ON SCREECHER

> HAWK
>
> Soon we'll have a real parrotberry pie
> with the eaglets buried in the crust.
> (CACKLES)

DISSOLVE TO:

INT. CAVE-DARKISH

WIDE ON PAPA YELLOW NAPE AND PICKLES
in bird cage.

In the distance, an opening to the cave shows the setting sun slipping below the horizon.

PAPA YELLOWNAPE

Hawks like to eat their parrots in the dark.

BRAINY

We've got to get outta here before

dinnertime.

The eaglets stick their heads out of PAPA' YELLOW NAPE'S and PICKLES'S pockets and begin to peep loudly for their mother.

CUT TO:

WIDE ON TOP OF BALD EAGLE MOUNTAIN

as the eagle perks up its head, hearing the loud peeps of its eaglets inside the yawning ravine.

FLEDGLING

What's that?

EAGLE

They said if they weren't back by sundown,

we must go and get them.

FLEDGLING

Hey, take it easy!

CLOSER ON EAGLE

FLEDGLING ties a knapsack and saddle on the EAGLE'S back.

The EAGLE lifts FLEDGLING up in its beak and takes off like a plane down the vertical cliffs and into the dark bowels of the cave. FLEDGLING hollers, but the EAGLE tosses him on his back

EAGLE

Hold on tight. A mother eagle will go

to any extreme to save its eaglets.

FLEDGLING

Just like a parrot!

WIDER ANGLE

SFX: Buzzing of a jet fighter plane, a loud drone as the eagle finally lands next to the bird cage, pushing up a cloud of
dust in its tracks. SFX: a screeching halt of a plane landing.

CLOSE ON PAPA YELLOW NAPE

PAPA YELLOW NAPE

Hurry and get this lock open.

We must get out before Hawk

returns for us.

PICKLES

When Hawk's bird's nest soup boils,

so do we.

WIDER ON EAGLE, PICKLES, PAPA YELLOW NAPE, and FLEDGLING

as the eagle pecks away at the lock, breaking it open.

The cage door springs open and PICKLES, PAPA YELLOW NAPE, and FLEDGLING speed away. SFX: We hear a peeping sound of chirps coming from the cage.
The EAGLE does a double take, perks up her head, tilts head
and runs back toward the cage, squawking.

EAGLE

My eaglets!

CLOSER ON PAPA YELLOW NAPE

PAPA YELLOW NAPE

Parrotoops! They must have fallen

from our pockets.

The EAGLE swoops up her eaglets and tucks them in a knapsack
on her back. They peer out of the sack and blink innocently,
peeping softly. The eagle stuffs the eaglets back inside the
pockets on the knapsack.

PAPA YELLOW NAPE and PICKLES mount the EAGLE's saddle and ride
away, up into the dark, reddish air of the caverns, dodging the many stalagmites
and stalactites as water drips from these limestone needles growing down from
the cave ceiling and up from the cave floor.

WIDE ON SWIMMING POOL ROOM-THE ATRIUM

as we get a view of the classical marble statues lined around the pool pointing to the way to freedom out of the cave, toward the light at the end of the cave.

CLOSER ON EAGLE

> EAGLE
>
> That awful Hawk made all these
>
> people into statues. Maybe your
>
> magical bracelet will also bring them
>
> back to life.

ANGLE ON ONE STATUE'S FACE

as a tear drop runs down its marble cheeks.

CLOSER ON PAPA YELLOW NAPE AND PICKLES

> PICKLES
>
> Let's give it a try. Give me that
>
> bracelet.

PICKLES takes the bracelet from Fledgling's outstretched wing and punches a white button on the bracelet. It lights up and pulsates for a moment. Then in an explosion of light, all the
statues are restored to life. The statues run free in all directions, cheering and shouting.

WIDER ON STATUES

as all statues with the exception of TWO scatter to the light at the end of the cave.

> STATUES
>
> (scattering wildly)
>
> We're free at last,

after all these years.

Let's head home for our village.

CLOSE ON THE ONE REMAINING PAIR OF MALE AND FEMALE STATUES

One marble statue runs over to greet PICKLES and PAPA YELLOW NAPE

MALE STATUE

Oh, thank you.

The last thing I remember

is that Hawk asked me to model

for his sculpture lesson.

WIDE ON FEMALE STATUE

as she runs towards EAGLE, PICKLES, PAPA YELLOW NAPE, and FLEDG-LING.

Then WIDER on FEMALE STATUE, PICKLES, FLEDGING, and EAGLE together.

CLOSER ON FEMALE STATUE as she embraces and kisses PICKLES in gratitude.

PICKLES makes a shy, cringing face and shows tense embarrassment.

TWO SHOT-STATUE AND PICKLES

FEMALE STATUE

I didn't realize that when Hawk

advertised for an interior decorator

that I'd be the decoration.

CLOSE ON FLEDGLING

FLEDGLING

It looks like this bracelet does

more than attract birds. It also

reverses all of Hawk's tricks.

I wonder what would happen if we

pointed it at Hawk and Screecher

and pressed this little blue button?

PAPA YELLOW NAPE

Not now, beaky bird.

WIDER on flying EAGLE

As she flaps her wings, creating high winds and a dust storm of many rainbow colors and flashing stars, whirling colors.

EAGLE soars. They fly out the mouth of the yawning ravine and into the bright blue air. HAWK sees them fly through the sky over his summer palace as he looks out of his kitchen window while stirring his pot of stew.

CUT TO:

WIDE SHOT

EXT. FLYING OVER THE ROOFTOPS AND TREE TOPS IN THE CLOUDS

CUT TO:

CLOSE on HAWK and SCREECHER who are sitting on the window sill looking at the flying EAGLE with PAPA YELLOW NAPE, FLEDGLING, and PICKLES on its back growing smaller as they head toward the Amazon village.

HAWK

Great hounds of hallucinations!

Get me Archy the archaeopteryx.

SFX: CLASH OF THUNDER and lightning.

As HAWK flings his curled fingers to cast a magical spell, in a cloud of pink smoke an archaeopteryx (ancient bird, half bird-half dinosaur or lizard bird) appears. It's all saddled
up and ready to fly.

WIDER ON HAWK, SCREECHER, AND ARCHY

HAWK

Come, Screecher, fly with me

on this dinosaur of birds.

Leap on this lizard, the

first bird that ever was.

CLOSE ON BIRD

SCREECHER leaps onto the archaeopteryx's back and snuggles into the saddle. HAWK flies up into the saddle and gives the reins a
few shakes.

WIDER ON BIRD, SCREECHER, HAWK

The bird takes off and follows the EAGLE who is now disappearing
o.s. beyond the horizon, out of shot. ARCHY has claws on its wings, teeth in its beak and more scales than feathers. It looks like a green, flying dragon of sorts with a horned crest on its pointy head. It's the same size and an equal match to the EAGLE.

CUT TO:

The sky chase begins. The Archy pursues and catches up to the EAGLE. EAGLE gains speed with ARCHY on its tail.

CLOSE ON ARCY

                              HAWK
                 Faster than a hawk could ever fly,

                 with dragon fire and bog mire.

HAWK points the way and steers the Archy.

WIDE on EAGLE

with ARCHY pursuing close behind. HAWK stretches out his fingers and zaps the eagle with a lightning bolt.

The bolt just misses PICKLES. He jumps out of his seat and begins to fall toward the ground. The ground comes up very fast as he tumbles earthward. EAGLE takes a dive as FLEDGLING holds onto his hat and swoops under PICKLES as PICKLES is scooped back into his saddle seat.

                              EAGLE
                 Whew! That was a close one.

                             PICKLES
                 A cool, blue eagle sure beats the

                 stress of doing my own flying in

                 this traffic.

CLOSE ON FLEDGLING

FLEDGLING whips out of his pocket his bird-attracting bracelet and buzzes the gold button. A parrot-shaped beak springs up from the bracelet shaped like a microphone. FLEDGLING speaks into the beak. Then he places the beak by his ear to receive a message. A parrot's voice squawks.

FLEDGLING

Calling all birds. Calling all birds.

PARROT (o.s.)

Awk! We've picked up a bogey

over the Parrotberry bush.

Send us a vector and we're

headed home.

FLEDGLING pushes a blue button on his bracelet. A light flashes.

WIDER ON BIRDS

Suddenly a travelling mound of black CROWS and toucans approach from the east. From the west a mountain of HAWKS approach the battle from the west, each aimed at a head-on collision with HAWK's flying dinosaur bird. These two humongous clouds of BIRDS both speed into shot at the same time with GARGAMEL caught in the middle as the two giant flocks of birds are headed for collision.

PICKLES

Look! Up in the sky.

It's every bird in the land.

PICKLES points to the tornado of birds, now turned into a cycloning whirlwind of two different flocks. Then that becomes four flocks, eight flocks. The entire sky fills with flocks of all different types of BIRDS.

CLOSER ON HAWK

He's still riding the ARCHY like it was some dragon horse with SCREECHER sitting on his shoulder.

HAWK grabs out of his saddle a lattice device with a spring. This is an expand-able device (like a forceps) that reaches across the clouds long enough to latch onto the tail of the EAGLE
flying fast just ahead of him.

WIDE ON EAGLE, PICKLES AND PAPA YELLOW NAPE

This expandable lattice-like device catches the EAGLE in mid-air. The jarring shakes PICKLES and PAPA YELLOW NAPE loose from the EAGLE'S back. PICKLES and PAPA YELLOW NAPE begin to fall again, plummeting almost to the Amazon Parrot Village below.
CLOSER ON THICK FLOCK OF GREEN PARROTS FORMING A MAGIC CARPET
WITH THEIR UNDULATING, FLAPPING FEATHERS

Just before they hit the tops of the trees a thick flock of TOUCANS suddenly rise from the Parrotberry Treetops and berry bushes and rise up to the occasion form-ing a thick crazyquilt of colored, feather carpet that allows PICKLES and PAPA YELLOW NAPE to float on this magical carpet of TOUCAN'S wings. The TOUCANS carry Parrotberries in their beaks as they head for home.

WIDER ON PICKLES and FLEDGLING

as they ride the carpet of toucans slowly floating to land in front of their own home.

CLOSER ON PICKLES, FLEDGLING, and PAPA YELLOW NAPE

PICKLES

We must help Eagle and her Eaglets.

FLEDGLING

Looks what's happening to Hawk.

The TOUCANS look skyward. PICKLES and FLEDGLING also look up to the clouds as the two armies of birds enclose HAWK in a tornado of a dark cloud of BIRDS.

The hawks begin to force apart the expandable lattice forceps and EAGLE flaps her wings and breaks free of the pinch.

PARETTE comes running from o.s. into shot.

PARETTE

Hi! Everybody. Look.

WIDER ON EAGLE

PARETTE points up at the sky.

PARETTE

The EAGLE is getting away.

Use the bird finder bracelet on Hawk's bird.

PICKLES presses the red button the the bracelet and it attracts all the birds toward the Amazon village and away from the EAGLE.
But the bracelet also attracts the bird HAWK's riding, the ARCHY.

CLOSER ON EAGLE

EAGLE has gotten out of the grips of the lattice-forceps expandable device and is gaining speed. All of a sudden the EAGLE turns and is attracted toward the AMAZON VILLAGE.

WIDE ON TWO ARMIES OF BIRDS

as the two armies of birds DO A DOUBLE TAKE and ATTACK one another. The HAWKS are now attacking the TOUCANS. The attacking birds DESERT HAWK. HAWK is now freed from the tornado of birds and is taking a nosedive straight for the Parrot's Amazon village.

FLEDGLING

You pressed the wrong button. We don't want

all those birds to land here and fight

one another. Try the blue button.

CLOSE ON PARETTE

PARETTE presses the bracelet's blue button as she aims at the ARCHY. Suddenly There is a beam of blue light filled with dancing rainbow colored soap bubbles.

WIDE ON BIRDS

As the beam reaches all the birds it fans out. Suddenly the birds go peaceful and chirp merrily. The have smiles on their beaks and a very mellow expression of peace and contentment on their faces.

The HAWKS fly to the east. The TOUCANS take to the west. The ARCHY is mellowed.

PULL BACK WIDER ON ARCHY

The mellow dinosaur-bird flaps its wings merrily and flies off back to HAWK'S castle.
DISSOLVE TO:

CLOSE ON HAWK

as he rides atop his mellow, happy ARCHY. The bird now sings the Parrot Song. The ARCHY flies in lazy circles over HAWK'S castle.

ARCHY

(sings his familiar song)

HAWK himself now has a large toucan's beak growing from his former smaller Hawk's beak.

                              HAWK

            What's this?

HAWK pulls at his new beak. Suddenly toucan's black and orange feathers sprout from HAWK'S clothes.

                              HAWK

            SCREECHER, get these feathers off of me.

HAWK pulls at his feathers as his pet iguana on his shoulder arches his back and growls at the bird feathers.

                           SCREECHER

            Rowrrr.

CUT TO:
WIDE ON PARETTE AND PICKLES

PARETTE, FLEDGLING, PAPA YELLOW NAPE, and PICKLES are riding on top of the EAGLE's back. They arrive at HAWK'S castle and confront him.

CLOSE ON HAWK

HAWK has now changed into a TOUCAN. He walks up to PARETTE.

                              HAWK

            Change me back and I'll promise anything.

                            PARETTE

            Will you stop sending those toucans to

            eat our Parrotberries?

HAWK

Yes. Yes. I'll do anything you want

only change me back.

I don't want to be Toco the toucan.

PARETTE

Here, have a Parrotberry pie.

PARETTE tosses the pie in his face.

HAWK has a temper tantrum as he wipes the pie from his face.

HAWK

Oh, you naughty Yellow Nape Amazon Parrot.

I'll have parrot pie for dessert tonight instead

of parrotberry turnover.

Suddenly he gets some pie in his mouth with his fingers and calms down fast.

HAWK

Hey, this pie is delicious.

SCREECHER

Magnificent!

PICKLES

So you see if you let our parrotberries grow,

you can eat pie this good all the time.

HAWK

Heh, heh, those toucans sure loved to eat

the special coating I sprayed on your

parrotberry crop. Actually toucans hate

parrotberries. Now change me back.

PICKLES

I'll change you back if you give me the formula

for removing your coating from our parrotberries.

HAWK grabs PARETTE and pulls the bracelet away. He clicks it on himselfs and turns back into his usual form.

HAWK locks PARETTE in the cookoo clock on his fireplace mantel. A wooden cookoo bird pops out of a small window on top of the clock and does its cookoo whistle, then returns. The Cookoo door closes. PARETTE bangs on the locked wooden door of the cookoo clock yelling for help.

SCREECHER leaps onto the ledge of the mantelpiece and menacingly sniffs at the PARROT behind the locked cookoo's door.

PARETTE

(muffled)

Help! Help!

The EAGLE charges into HAWK. But HAWK hits the pink button on the bracelet and the EAGLE is transformed into a tiny eaglet that peeps loudly for help.

EAGLET

Peep. Peep. Peep.

PICKLES sweeps up the eaglet and tosses her into his pocket as he runs for his life. HAWK chases after him. HAWK points and motions to SCREECHER. The iguana runs to hunt down PICKLES. HAWK rubs his wings in circles and paces in anticipation.

HAWK

Screecher! How about parrot and eaglet

over a bed of noodles?

(rubbing his beak and wings in circles)

Hmmm…I can already hear the sizzle before

I've seen the steak.

CLOSE ON SHADOWS OF SCREECHER AND PICKLES

SCREECHER makes a leap from a tall fireplace mantel to pounce on PICKLES below who is now corned against a wall. We see the elongated dark shadow of SCREECHER in slow motion in the act of pouncing on PICKLES who stands against the wall. CAMERA SHOT on the two shadows.

While in midair, quickly PICKLES pulls out of his trousers pocket his MAGI-CAL SALT SHAKER (which he used before to sprinkle on the Parrotberries) to chase away the parrots. Now he tosses a sprinkle of golden salt into SCREECHER'S face and a black cloud of awful smelling smoke engulfs and twines about SCREECHER as HAWK comes into the shot from o.s. to come to SCREECHER'S aid.

The cloud kicks up a big stink around SCREECHER. A white stripe forms and runs down the center of SCREECHER's blackening reptile body so that SCREECHER looks just like a skunk. SCREECHER growls and draws back with his tail between his legs, in embarrassment at how stinky he smells.

PICKLES

Now that's what I call smelling salts.

HAWK reacts to the awful stink cloud surrounding SCREECHER. He holds his nose and winces.

HAWK

Peeeuuuu! You smell like a skunk.

WIDER ON PICKLES and HAWK

PICKLES laughs at his own joke as HAWK grabs him in his fist by his feet dangling upside down as HAWK walks to his kitchen.

PICKLES

Help. Put me down.

SCREECHER tries to jump into HAWK'S arms while he's dangling PICKLES. But HAWK shoos him away, holding his nose.

HAWK

Go take a bath, Screecher!

CUT TO:

SCREECHER runs off and jumps in a washtub of water. Clothes that were soaking in the washtub go flying through the air.

CUT TO.
WIDE ON HAWK'S KITCHEN

HAWK carries PICKLES upside down into his kitchen. He sits him down on a serving plate on his table and begins to arrange mushrooms around the platter with PICKLES sitting up in the middle.

CLOSE ON PICKLES AND HAWK IN THE KITCHEN

HAWK

It's parrot pie for dinner,

my friend, stuffed with mushrooms

a la King and cloves. (CACKLE)

HAWK stuffs a clove into a mushroom and then stuffs it into PICKLES's mouth.

With his hands free, PICKLES tosses some golden granules from his magical salt-shaker into HAWK'S face.

PICKLES

It's the seasoning to be jolly.

La, la la la la, la la la la.

HAWK RUBS HIS EYES AND SNEEZES.

Suddenly HAWK becomes mellow and peaceful. A silly smile appears on his face as he changes into a giant mushroom stuffed with cloves sitting on an "island" wedge of pie crust .

WIDER ON PICKLES

PICKLES climbs down the table leg and runs along the kitchen floor past SCREECHER who's still splashing in the washtub of water with the wet clothes laying all around the tub on the floor.

PICKLES passes SCREECHER and bravely calls to him as PICKLES continues walking out of shot.

CLOSER ON PICKLES

PICKLES

That should keep him mushroomed on an island

until dinner time.

CLOSE ON PARETTE AND PICKLES

PICKLES climbs up the curtain sashweight and drapery cords until he reaches the top OF THE MANTELPIECE\FIREPLACE. He breaks open the cookoo clock wooden door with a pencil lying in front of him and out rides PARETTE sitting astride the wooden cookoo yellow bird as the clock chimes. COOKOO, COOKOO, COOKOO. She jumps off the cookoo bird as the bird goes back inside the clock and the door closes.

> PARETTE
>
> What happened?

> PICKLES
>
> You remember that special salt shaker
>
> that didn't stop the toucans from
>
> eating our fruit?

> PARETTE
>
> Don't tell me it stopped Hawk.

> PICKLES
>
> It has the odor of success.

ANGLE ON PICKLES AND PARETTE

PICKLES and PARETTE climb down the drapery cords and sashweight to the floor.

PARETTE whips out her magical bracelet.

> PARETTE
>
> The Eagle!

PARETETE clicks the blue button and the eaglet in PICKLES's pocket peeps twice, swells and bursts through his pocket, it's muscles growing until it reaches full size standing on the floor.

CLOSE ON EAGLE

EAGLE

C'mon, let's get outta here!

WIDER ON PICKLES, PARETTE, EAGLE AND SCREECHER

PICKLES and PARETTE leap onto the EAGLE's back just as SCREECHER runs into the room and leaps does a double take when he sees how large and ferocious the eagle looks.

EAGLE

Stay back, Screecher, unless you

want to star in my iguana pie.

EAGLE flaps her wings and flies out breaking through the wooden shutters on the windows. Wood pieces fly over the heads of PICKLES and PARETTE as they duck. SCREECHER recoils in his tracks, coming to a screeching halt. He watches them take off.
PICKLES turns around as they soar, yelling back through his cupped hands to SCREECHER.

PICKLES

Don't worry about Hawk. He'll

be back to his old self by dinner.

So don't eat that old stuffed mushroom

sitting in the kitchen.

DISSOLVE TO:

EXT.-A BRIGHT, LEAFY DAY-AMAZON VILLAGE

WIDE on FLEDGLING, GRANDPA MACAW, NESTLING, EAGLE, PICK-LES, PARETTE, and PAPA YELLOW NAPE.

> GRANDPA MACAW
>
> Welcome back, my parrots.
>
> You've saved our tasty
>
> berries from the toucans.

CLOSE ON EAGLE

> EAGLE
>
> And look what I have here.

EAGLE pulls out from under its wing a vial of formula.

ANGLE ON NESTLING, PICKLES, and EAGLE

NESTLING sniffs the vial of liquid.

> NESTLING
>
> Why, it's Hawk's secret formula
>
> for distracting toucans from our Parrotberries.

> PICKLES
>
> What is it?

> EAGLE
>
> (laughing)
>
> Oil of eagle.

ANGLE ON PAPA YELLOW NAPE, PARETTE, PICKLES, and HATCH-LING

PARETTE

It was so simple.

The scent of big birds always

frightens away the smaller birds.

PICKLES

Then we don't need those

magical salts that make our

fruit bitter.

PICKLES takes out his salt shaker and gives it to PAPA YELLOW NAPE.

PARETTE takes out her magical bracelet.

PARETTE

And we don't need this bracelet

to attract any more toucans.

PARETTE bends down and hands it to HATCHLING who's crawling into the shot from o.s. HATCHLING takes the bracelet in his mouth and PEEPS.

HATCHLING

Peep. Google. Burble.

HATCHLING puts the bracelet on his own wrist and crawls away into GRANDPA MACAW'S arms. GRANDPA MACAW lifts HATCHLING onto his shoulder.

CLOSE ON FLEDGLING.

as he takes the two eaglets out from under his wing and hands them to EAGLE.

FLEDGLING

I've got my parrotlings and now here's

your eaglets, safe, sound, and well-fed.

ANGLE ON EAGLE, PAPA YELLOW NAPE, and FLEDGLING

EAGLE takes her two eaglets and kisses them, hugging them warmly. A rainbow of colors light up the blue sky and white clouds.

PAPA YELLOW NAPE

Before you go, would you like to see

the birdfeeder in our own garden?

EAGLE

(smiling)

No, I've got to get my eaglets back

to the nest. But I don't know how to

thank you for saving my eaglets.

PAPA YELLOW NAPE

And I don't know how to thank you

for saving Hatchling.

EAGLE

Well, there's one gift I can give you.

FLEDGLING

What's that?

CLOSE ON EAGLE AND PICKLES

EAGLE takes out a Parrotberry pie from his knapsack and hands it to PICKLES.

EAGLE

I managed to salvage your last Parrotberry

pie from Hawk's oven.

WIDER ON EAGLE and PICKLES

PICKLES

Beakadoodle. Thanks.

EAGLE

And there's one more present,

for Hyacinth.

HYACINTH hurries into the shot from o.s.

ANGLE ON HYACINTH

HYACINTH

That pie is the last

unless I replace all those

Parrotberry trees and bushes

the toucans ate down to the roots.

EAGLE

Don't worry.

EAGLE takes two draw string purses from his knapsack on his back.

ANGLE ON EAGLE and HYACINTH

EAGLE

Here's Hawk's last bag of

seeds, one for the trees, and the other

for the bushes.

HYACINTH

I'll be able to replant for the spring.

I don't know how to thank you either.

HYACINTH hugs EAGLE and gives him a kiss on the beak.

EAGLE

So long, Yellow Napes and Macaws.

EAGLE shakes wings with HYACINTH. EAGLE flaps her wings and soars. She circles low once, swooping down to echo one more message as she hovers in midair.

EAGLE

Just keep the hunters off of the

top of Bald Eagle Mountain.

ANGLE ON PICKLES

PICKLES

(waving to Eagle)

Sure thing. Everybody knows

eagles taste awful.

WIDER ON EAGLE IN SKY

EAGLE soars again

until the bird becomes a black dot on top of the mountain's peak.

FADE OUT TO THE END.

Chapter Five

Writing Cartoon Scripts for Younger Children

When writing for younger children, animated cartoon scripts can be adapted and revised for puppeteers to present in a puppet theater setting. Techniques of writing scripts for cartoon animation also work well when writing life story or personal history scripts. The practice writing springboards, premises, and several drafts polishes your ability to present the highlights of a life story with cartoon animated characters in your computer or online, on disk, or on video. All you have to do is substitute the real person or real personality for the cartoon character, avatar, or robot online, on video, and on disk.

You can write your life story or personal history as an animated cartoon, design animated computer games, including writing the scripts, or think creatively "outside the box." Back in the nineties, writing a life story sometimes featured 'avatars' or computer-generated persona 'robots' online.

Hypertext fiction and life stories flummoxed many in the mid-nineties, but opened new channels of creative expression online. What other media can you use for your life story time capsules? Feature the highlights of significant events in your own life or rites of passage. Keepsakes include your personal journal, video clips and photos, along with DNA-driven genealogy—for-ancestry reports.

How to Write Life Stories as "Saturday-Morning-Type" Cartoons & How to Write Cartoon Animation Scripts for Multimedia Markets

"You watch cartoons all morning six days a week? I know you're around 70, maybe. Is that what all older folks, or 'spent' people watch?" The audience waited to hear my answer as an obviously older person speaking from the panel to a teenage conference attendee.

"Why do you watch them?" I answered. "I stop the frame and study the timing before I write plays for puppeteers or for the animation script markets. It's good research to look at the action in the frame before I write the dialogue or direction." I find taking apart the action at the basic level helps a writer see how to approach a scene. The movement, dialogue, and direction from animation convey a sense of lighting and contrast for a small area like a live stage. It helps a writer break down dialogue into shorter sentences and cleaner paragraphs.

Writing animation is tougher than writing live-action or dialogue in first person diary novels. You want to put stretch marks on your wallet? Then call every shot in an animation script. You have up to two lines of dialogue before you have to change the shot, the frame, that is. Shot changed already? Then start describing the scene all over again along with what action is happening.

There's no director in animation that will put in the camera angles on your script or other directions. No one will stage your action other than you. Here's your chance to play master of your universe and do everything as the writer in 37-59 pages for a half-hour script that actually runs only 22 minutes.

An animation script takes twice as much writing as a live action screen play. You write two pages of animation for each screen minute. Saturday morning cartoons are the ultimate in teaching tools when transferred to personal history or life stories and to other educational and training materials. Many writers in animation entered the field decades ago by first writing half-hour television commercials for toys and related educational devices.

Record Cartoons for Study and Analysis

Instead of merely watching cartoons on your TV, record them to tape or DVD. If you're working with tape, stop your VCR machine and freeze a frame. Now write down all the action occurring in that freeze-frame. It should have a beginning, middle, and end—same as in a short story. Put in one line of dialogue. Practice until you become familiar with finding the beginning, middle, and end—the "short story" theme in each freeze-frame. Do you understand what you're looking for—the story line, the action in each frame of animation?

Watch tapes as often as three times a day until the action in each frame becomes familiar as a story with a beginning, middle, and end. There is gold in animation festivals, whether you're writing animation to entertain or writing personal histories in animation format as a way to use your creative expression or as the cliché goes "think outside the box."

Cartoon writers of the eighties and nineties lived in a hypercubed universe where thinking was done in three dimensions. Today it's action, effects, and visual writing. Only it goes beyond thinking in three dimensions. You have to think inside out. Write in sound effects and write visually. Animation writing is an exercise in highly technical visual thinking. You form a team with the skilled computer artist-animator-designer and the computer engineer.

Learn from TV Toy Ads

Saturday morning cartoons are there to sell toys to children (and parents) who must be persuaded either by their children or by the cartoon ad itself. Watch for the commercials. Sponsors pay for them. Writers can work at the educational materials end of the animation market, write ad copy and dialogue with action for the sponsors, or write the animation for entertainment.

There's another inroad—writing personal life stories and histories, even corporate histories, as animation scripts and illustrated novels. On video or DVD, the animation action and script work together to showcase the highlights of a person's life at any age....or a company's success stories. It all can be a cartoon either for the story itself or to sell as an advertisement, educational materials or a product.

Foreign Animation

In the eighties, when animation began to be sent overseas to be designed, script writers often turned to computer game design and computer game script writing as one alternative. Today many universities have impacted graphic design majors in schools of new media. Computer animation in a variety of countries is shown on TV everywhere. Have you seen the last computer animation from Japan, for example?

What about the 'anime' field and independent producers of animation stories? You could offer animation online and on disk portraying children's life stories for birthday gifts and rites of passage ceremonies. There are so many applications to writing life stories as animation scripts. Only you need a computer animator to be on your team, someone to design the animation art and do the computer editing.

To study animation script writing, hunt for the old cartoon scripts of the thirties and forties. They're rare vintages. Keep a tape or DVD library of dozens of old-time radio programs. Join old-time radio and video clubs online where you can exchange or rent these old cartoons on DVDs or CDs.

Listen to old-time radio shows such as Captain Midnight and The Shadow. Can you write a radio play of someone's life story or personal history in that format—old time radio with special sound effects? If so, put it on a DVD or CD and up on a streaming Web site. That's one way to create a time capsule, keepsake album, or personal and corporate history.

Watch cartoon animation from other lands. Look at the World War II cartoons shown in local theaters in the forties. They are now on DVDs and on VHS tapes. When the tapes deteriorate with time, they are transferred to higher quality DVDs and whatever comes next. Look at the WW 2 themes in the cartoon animation, such as Donald Duck fighting Nazis.

For a personal historian, looking at cartoons from other countries at different times can help you learn how propaganda cartoons were used because people thought them to be patriotic. At different periods in history, foreign governments paid for propaganda cartoons that often turn up in archives and libraries. Look at your own country's cartoons from years ago. Was the theme patriotic? In what ways? What did the themes emphasize here, teamwork, for example.

You can make a hobby or research project out of studying the world of animation script writing during various wars, in time, or in geographic space around the world. The themes go beyond the design of animation or the script writing. There are patterns and values in some of these cartoons.

What stories do they tell? What values and virtues? Do they have a purpose, mission, crusade, slogan, proverb, or other message? How do the cartoons impact people, and how do people impact cartoon animation and script writing?

How to Enter the Field of Cartoon Animation Script Writing or Animation of Life Stories and Personal Histories

You can start by either researching the needs of animation design companies or advertising agencies that sponsor the Saturday morning cartoons. Many writers were spiraled into animation script writing from spin-offs of advertising agency electronic ad copywriting and/or graphic illustration jobs.

Some entered animation script writing as former comic-book artists or writers. Others were live-action scriptwriters. Some also are computer game designers.

You have the animation artist-designer who turns to script writing. And you have the computer engineer interested in game design.

The animation script writer needs the soul of an illustrator even if you don't do visual art work. You can paint pictures with visual writing. The pictures would emphasize action and dialogue. The best way to train is to study paintings in art galleries and museums and watch cartoon animation for exercising the visual side.

On the writing side, you look at cartoon animation scripts and analyze them for story, length, action, dialogue, and appeal to the audience and age level. You also find out whether the script will sell toys or other educational materials and products advertised between the cartoons.

Toy Marketing

Life stories and corporate histories can be marketed as toys, board games, or computer games. Know what age level you'll be targeting. You can even write story books using the lives of your clients who could be children if the parents give information and specify what kind of life story book or cartoon they want with the 'avatar' or "robot image" or photograph of their child.

You work out with the parent what kind of educational life story approach you want to take with animation and script with the family. It makes a fascinating birthday party presentation and gift. From lives to grand openings of stores, you are marketing a toy or a life story with animation script and design.

Between 1984 and 1986 a flood of animation began being turned out for syndication. Through the advertising agency route, animation writers trained on the job to sell toys and women's products. They wrote copy for advertisements and animation scripts. Animation writers marketed toys to children and skin care products primarily to women. The animated script had to sell shampoo, detergents, and bake mixes.

Artists became writers, and writers trained in animation design. Add that group of creative people to a farrago of Hollywood script writers seeking more work or alternatives. Many script writers with degrees in screenwriting turned to the Saturday morning cartoons to make a living. College campuses began to offer courses in animation and later, new media animation such as desktop video animation and new media writing.

The Boom and the Bust

A tremendous amount of animation flooded the markets around 1986. By 1987, the boom turned to bust, leaving many writers by 1988 vying for what assignments and contracts came their way by the time the Internet brought new hope to the nineties and beyond. The good news is that those who had been writing animation scripts leaped into writing live-action screen plays or went into multimedia educational design and writing. Others went into Web design and online digital journalism. Still others sought out print-on-demand publishing venues.

Breaking into cartoon animation can take one to five years. Collaboration is common. Often you find work through the multimedia and other computer-related markets. I found work as an independent contractor writing success stories and case histories for a software manufacturer at the end of the nineties. There is a bright side.

Animation Writing Agents

Since writing animation pays no residuals, newcomers are given a second chance if they get the go-ahead to write a sample script. Prime-time TV won't touch you without an agent. So without an agent, you need to pitch a few seconds in writing to a story editor at your chosen animation studio.

You first phone the various studios and independent producers and ask for the name of the story editor. Then you talk to the story editor or pitch in writing. It's the story editor who has the power to work with you and is your first link to the industry. First you have to pitch a story, and most often the story line is related to the cartoon show's 'bible.' The 'bible' is a reference and resource book of what the characters are like and what they do in a particular cartoon show on TV.

If you live out of town from where the studio is located, tell the story editor that you have a computer and can send the script electronically. It can go by email. Most studios have bulletin boards to which you can download or upload all types of pitches, springboards, treatments, stories, and scripts.

Telecommuting

The computer bulletin board for animation writers in the 1980s was called "The Algonquin Board." Its private number and mailing address appealed to members because the only way to become a member was to have someone in the industry recommend you.

You were in a position that sometimes the only way in was to accept an assignment on speculation and then ask your story editor to recommend you as a member. Otherwise, you were left to introduce yourself at professional meetings by volunteering for such types of organizations.

Today, you can check out the many associations and unions for animation writers that are listed online. Network with the many associations listed as links at: The Electronic Media and Film major Web site of Towson University, Electronic Media & Film Department, 8000 York Rd. Towson, MD 21252-0001 http://www.towson.edu/emf/links.htm

What you want to look for on bulletin and message boards or email lists of related associations are job information, marketing ideas, and professional resources. Join associations and volunteer to interview people. Write articles for the association's newsletter or other publications. Mailing lists and bulletin boards online may have job information and valuable resources. Meet people and find out whether they want to spread the news about what they are doing in the field. Write success stories.

Meet other writers and story editors at trade and professional associations in the field of writing for animation. Back in the eighties, there was a bulletin board that served live-action screenwriters called the Wicked Scherzo Board, but back then, the only way to get phone numbers of members was to ask a member in the industry to recommend you.

You need not have sold a script at that time. Today, most networking is done in various universities departments of electronic media and film with industry internships and professional associations as members volunteer to work on newsletters and at conventions and conferences to 'network.'

Instead of meeting only writers, try to network with musicians, artists, engineers, special effects designers, and technicians who work in the computer animation industry. It's all about teamwork, and every artist needs a script to animate. Check out the advertising agencies, educational publishers and producers, trainers, corporate industrial film producers, and comic book publishers for their writing needs.

Then there are the radio scripts for Internet broadcast or multicast. Elementary school teachers can use plays for puppet shows as well as the producers of the puppet shows for schools. Everyone works with some kind of script presenting to students or at weddings and other celebrations, and scripts have themes or niche markets. Also try the ethnic and religious markets.

Working with Nets

One way to meet people in the animation and script writing industries is to join the International Animated Film Association (ASIFA). The Web site is at: http://www.swcp.com/animate/. Email address is: asifa@asifa.org. There are national and international chapters.

The Los Angeles headquarters of ASIFA can help you reach people employed at the various studios in the vicinity of Hollywood. Call the studios directly and speak to the story editors. Check the *Encyclopedia of Associations* in your public library for a long list of animation associations worldwide or look on the Web at www.google.com or other search engines for more associations. Some offer workshops with networking. Stay in communication with the various studios in Los Angeles.

Call the story editors each month, and ask them to send you animation scripts. You can write to them and enclose self-addressed stamped envelopes. Never pester them or call too frequently. Bring to the story editors your related stories and your unique scripts. To prepare, read the animation scripts. Analyze the scripts. Study the scripts to see what was emphasized and find out why those scripts were accepted and satisfactory. Those topics give you factual material to discuss with the story editors.

As story editors to send you the 'bibles' of various animation characters you select. This 'bible' is a book several inches thick that tells everything you need to know about the cartoon character. If you write life stories as cartoon animation, then you'll need to make such a 'scrap book' or 'bible' on the person about whose life you are writing.

Learn all you can about the cartoon character and his henchmen from the cartoon bible. Make yourself valuable to studio officials. Ask them what already has been pitched. Ask what titles have sold the quickest. Ask kids what makes them laugh. Ask older adults what makes them laugh. Ask kids what they want to see on television cartoons. Ask people of all ages what they would like to see of their own life stories on TV cartoons, even if the TV set is from their own DVD disk of their life story or other significant event.

Ask the story editor what are the taboos. The bible and sample scripts will let you know in general, but if you miss a point, ask. There are several types of cartoon shows on TV, the hard and the soft.

Hard and Soft TV Animation Shows

There are soft and hard cartoon animation shows on TV. Soft shows don't have too much action adventure. Write sample scripts of each type. The hard shows have the "hit 'em hard" characters that enjoy things that people can't do legally.

Do you really enjoy your characters torching toy stores as in the cartoon, *Robocop*? Or would you prefer to go inward into your imagination and write a zoo story? Look at scripts from the soft animation shows produced during the eighties such as Jim Henson's *Muppet Babies*.

You might want to watch the old cartoons and compare the action on screen with the written script. The scripts often are available from the story editors, animation writers' associations, and also from stores in Hollywood that sell old scripts. In the eighties when I was writing sample animation scripts, the story editors from the various studios sent me their 'bible' and sample scripts for various shows.

Chances are no one will buy your sample scripts. You might want to focus writing life story scripts to be later put into computer animation with a variety of animation software. Sample scripts for particular shows that no one buys are not a total waste. They are used as part of your resume.

You show a story editor your sample script along with your resume. These samples show the story editors that you know the format. You learn to format a story, and you learn to structure a story. It's one way to showcase your 'handle' on credible cartoon dialogue.

Pitching

Introduce yourself by phone to the story editor. Find out whether they also take email queries. It's more personal by phone if not in person. Tell the story editor that you have a sample script to send. Give your verbal pitch in 20 seconds.

Then tell the story editor that you'll send the required written pitch. Find out whether they want the pitch emailed or sent by regular mail.

The story editor will probably say your idea has been pitched. However, if your story line has a fresh angle, you'll me asked to mail it in. Here's your chance to be creative and still stick to the 'bible' or script requirements for a particular show.

Springboard

You first send the story editor a half-page, double-spaced bare-bones summary called a springboard. Every story can be pared to a half-page bare bones summary. Look at it as if it were the marketing material that goes on the back cover of your story.

Think of the springboard as the back-cover marketing description of your novel designed to hook the reader. It is there to make the story editor want to open your book or actually read more of your script. You will not be paid to write a springboard.

After you have written this half-page double-spaced springboard containing the bare bones of your script or story, you will be asked to write a premise. So, if the editor likes your springboard and assigns you a premise to write, you will be paid for the premise.

Premise

A premise is a two-page, double-spaced, expanded springboard. Make your premise a story with a beginning, middle, and end. Every frame and sequence of your story needs a beginning, middle, and end. Your premise needs to contain the hook that the story editor will use to sell your idea to the networks or to clients.

Cartoons have paid advertising sponsors. They are aired to sell the sponsor's toys. The most important point that can sell your episode for a Saturday morning cartoon is its title.

Work on your title to make it salable. If you're writing a life story as an animation script for use on DVDs or computers, keep the title pertinent and short. Often familiar titles sell well, especially in first editions.

Give your play, skit, animation script, or dramatization of a life story event a title that makes an impact. Example: Murphy's Law is familiar. Choose something similarly familiar to most people for your title.

Titles that resemble popular, ageless songs also sell. Talk to your story editor about what is expected or taboo in the title. Look at the best hundred titles that have sold cartoons. What does the story editor or clients like about those titles?

Outline

Once the network or client approves your premise, you will be paid to write an outline. Be specific. Break the action down frame by frame and scene by scene. Use hardly any dialogue at all. Your outline runs between eight and 12 pages in length if you are writing for a half-hour show—which is actually only 22 minutes of screen time.

First Draft

When the story editor approves your outline, you move to the first draft of your script. There's always the first draft followed by the revisions. There may be one or two writers assigned to the script. One writer may be credited with the story and one or two more with the script.

Bumped Off

Before you agree to write any material for pay, you'll be handed a "work for hire" agreement to sign. At any stage, you may be "bumped off." That means being cut off with no more pay or credits. Once you are cut off by the studio it can give your premise or outline to any other writer or shelve your work permanently. You could be paid for your premise and then cut off. Or this could happen as you hand in your outline, in which case you'll be paid for the outline.

How Much?

Payments vary with each studio. Some pay 40 percent of the script fee if you're cut off at outline. The minimum fee for a half-hour script at several studies started at slightly more than $3,000. For network shows, payment could range from $4,000 to $6,000 or more, depending upon your experience.

What Are You Worth?

Make yourself valuable to studio officials. Ask them what has been pitched in the past. Ask what titles sold the quickest. Talk to children. Ask kids what makes them laugh. Send studios a collection or database of children's reactions to cartoons when you are asking for work. A child's creativity has not been discouraged by rejection. Children don't have writer's block. Comic strip writers, filmmakers, teachers, and anthropologists also can be resources.

Research Comic Books

Many former writers of comic book stories and similar novels have become animation script writers. Talk to the people who write and draw the comic books and their publishers and editors. Many cartoon shows are based on comic-book or comic-strip heroes and heroines. Some scripts are spin-offs of live action TV programs. The eighties saw Robocop and Star Trek take off in a variety of media from novels to cartoons. Animation writing is a collaborative effort. Firms that publish comic books also may have animation studios on the opposite coast.

Animation Scripts Use Comic-Book Style Dialogue and Descriptive Language

The same descriptive language used in comic strips is written into animation scripts. For example, you'll see the heavy use of sound effects (SFX) in most lines of description and dialogue in adventure-action cartoons. Animation scripting is mostly description of action and hardly any dialogue at all.

Comic Conventions

Attend the comic conventions in your sit, and sit on the "writing for animation" panel. Create your own panel at conferences and conventions for people in similar industries. Phone and write to experts you will be researching or interviewing for articles you may write in a newsletter of one of the trade or professional associations.

Ask the experts to come and join you on a panel at a convention or conference or a class or group meeting. An example would be a writer's club or a film society. The topic could be on how to write for the animation industry.

Comic Books

Life stories can be presented as comic books. That's one alternative. Another is writing for the animation industry or speaking about that industry by researching comic books. Talk to people who work at home with computer and Internet connection writing cartoon scripts. Ask these experts to be on your panel at conferences such as comic book publishers' conventions or seminars on writing for the new media.

Timing Is Important

Most cartoon shows are picked up by studios in February. Call various studios during the month when they are pitching network shows. Exceptions to the February pickup rule included the old 1980s shows such as *The Smurfs* (Hanna-Barbera) and *Fraggle Rock* or the *Muppet Babies* (Marvel) which had early pickups. *Alf* was produced at Disney Studios in Burbank, California. There were a wide variety of shows a decade ago such as Pee Wee's Playhouse. What about today? More life stories in caricature, like South Park and the Simpsons of the new millennium.

The persons in charge of development (as well as the producers) are listed in the credits that roll at the end of each cartoon show. Record the cartoons for your personal research and find out who is the appropriate person to query regarding writing springboards or other materials. Sometimes a producer needs public relations material written. That's another side door into the industry, through public relations work on the cartoon shows or with the sponsors. Multimedia animation studies are another door that may offer internships.

The mid-eighties was one of the "golden ages" of Saturday morning cartoon shows on TV when freelance script writers had the chance to walk in and present their writing to story editors or to telephone from anywhere. You didn't necessarily have had to live in Los Angeles to be a cartoon script writer. Today with Internet multimedia, you can produce life stories or corporate histories yourself and present them as animated cartoon shows or other types of multimedia presentations such as time capsules.

What you need to search for is the 'downtime' at the studios of your choice. That downtime is a good time to talk to story editors about writing sample scripts, obtaining 'bibles' and other materials you'll need to begin your springboard for a particular show. Your one best sample script can be used to sell many shows at several studios.

Chapter Six

What Makes a Life Story Highlight Salable as a One-Act Play or Skit?

"Celebration of Life" Plays and Skits Based on Interviewing and Taping

People are "less camera shy" when two from the same peer group or class pair up and interview each other on video camcorder or on audio tape from a list of questions rehearsed. People also can write the questions they want to be asked and also write out and familiarize themselves with the answers alone and/or with their interviewers from their own peer group.

Some people have their favorite proverbs, or a logo that represents their outlook on life. Others have their own 'crusade' or mission. And some have a slogan that says what they are about in a few words…example, "seeking the joy of life," or "service with a smile."

A play can come from someone's slogan, for example. A slogan, logo, proverb, or motto can form the foundation for a questionnaire on what they want to say in an oral history or personal history video or audio tape on in a multimedia presentation of their life story highlights. Here are some ways to interview people for personal history time capsules or how to inspire them to interview one another in a group setting or in front of a video camcorder in private with only interviewer and interviewee present.

And then there are those who want to tape themselves alone in their room or office with a camcorder on a tripod and a remote control device or a tape recorder and photographs. When records stop, there are always the DNA-driven geneal-ogy and ancestry printouts.

Some people enjoy writing their life stories more than they like to speak about it. Or they prefer to read from a script as an audio tape. For those whose voices are impaired or for those who prefer to let a synthetic software voice tell their story, I recommend software such as TextAloud. This software allows anyone to cut and paste their writing from a disk such as a floppy disk, CD, DVD, or hard drive disk to the TextAloud software and select the type of voice to read their writing. With AT&T Natural Voices, you can select a male or female voice.

There are also voices with accents, such as a British accent male voice, and voice software available in a variety of languages to read writing in other lan-guages. TextAloud is made by Nextup.com at the Web site: http://www.nextup.com/. According to their Web site, "TextAloud MP3 is Text-to-Speech software that uses voice synthesis to create spoken audio from text. You can listen on your PC or save text to MP3 or wave files for listening later." I play the MP3 files on my MP3 player.

I save the files to a CD as MP3 files. In this way I can turn my writing into audio books, pamphlets, or articles, poetry, plays, monologues, skits, or any form of writing read aloud by the synthetic software voice software. I save my audio files as MP3 files so I can play my personal history audio in my MP3 player on in my personal computer. MP3 files are condensed and take up a lot less room in your computer or on a Web site or CD and DVD disk than an audio .wav file.

For people who are creating "celebration of life" oral or personal history audio tapes, it works well especially for those who prefer not to read their own writing aloud to a tape recorder. Although most people would like to hear their relatives' voices on tape in audio and video, some people are not able to read their works aloud to a recorder or camcorder.

The synthetic voices will turn any type of writing saved on a disk as a text file into recorded voice—from short poetry to long-length books. The voices are usu-ally recorded with Total Recorder software and saved as an MP3 file so they can be played on MP3 players or on most computers with CD players.

For those taping persons live in video to make time capsules or other keepsake albums in voice and/or video, it's best to let people think what they are going to say by handing them a list of a few questions. If you're working with a group of older adults, let one of the group members interview another group member by asking each question from a list of several questions.

If you give someone a week's notice to come up with an answer to each ques-tion from a list of ten questions and give them two minutes to respond to each question by discussing how it relates to events in their lives or their experiences, you have a twenty minute video tape.

If you allow only a minute for each question from a list of thirty questions, you have a thirty-minute tape. Times may not be exact as people tend to elaborate to flesh out a question. Let the interview and interviewee practice before recording. So it's good to pair up two people. One will ask the interview questions, and the other will answer, talking about turning points and significant events in their lives.

They can be asked whether they have a personal proverb or slogan they live by or a motto or personal logo. Tapes can be anywhere from a half hour to an hour for life stories that can be saved as an MP3 file to a CD. Other files such as a Wave file (.wav) take up too much space on a CD. So they could be condensed into an MP3 file and saved that way. TextAloud and Total Recorder are software programs that save audio files. You can also use Music Match to convert .wav files to MP3 files.

I use TextAloud software and Total Recorder. Also I save the files as MP3 files for an audio CD that will also go up on a Web site. I use Windows Media Player to play the video files and save them as a Windows Media file (WMV file) so they can be easily uploaded to a Web site and still play in Windows Media Player that comes with Windows XP software.

When making time capsules in multimedia, I save on a CD and/or a DVD, and upload the file from my hard disk to a Web site. Copies of the CDs can be given to relatives, the interviewee, museums, libraries, and various schools who may be interested in oral history with a theme.

The themes can be celebrations of life, living time capsules, or fit into any group theme under an umbrella title that holds them together. This can be an era, such as living memories of a particular decade, life experiences in oral history of an area in geography, an ethnic group, or any other heading. Or the tapes can be of individuals or family groups. Not only life stories, but poetry, plays, novels, stories, and any other form of creative nonfiction or fiction writing can be recorded by synthetic voices as audio story or book collections. Some work well as children's stories and other types of writings as life stories or poetry.

Themes can vary from keepsake albums to time capsules to collections of turning points in history from the life stories of individuals. Also, themes can be recorded as "old time radio" programs or as oral military history from the experiences of veterans and notated to the Veterans History Project at the Library of Congress or other groups and museums. Make sure you have signed *release forms* that also release you from liability should any problems arise from putting someone's life story and name on the Web and/or donating it to a library or other public archive.

A good example of a release form is the one posted at the Veteran's History Project Web site where life stories of veterans are donated to the Library of

Congress and accessible to the public for educational or scholarly research. Check out the .PDF release forms for both the interviewer and the interviewee at their Web site. The release form for veterans is at: http://www.loc.gov/folklife/vets/vetform-vetrelease.pdf.

Chapter Seven

Writing the Recorded Experiences of Older Adults into Plays, Skits, or Monologues

When High-School Students Interview Older Adults

STEP 1: Send someone enthusiastic about personal and oral history to senior community centers, lifelong learning programs at universities, nursing homes, or senior apartment complexes activity rooms. You can reach out to a wide variety of older adults in many settings, including at libraries, church groups, hobby and professional or trade associations, unions, retirement resorts, public transportation centers, malls, museums, art galleries, genealogy clubs, and intergenerational social centers.

STEP 2: Have each personal historian or volunteer bring a tape recorder with tape and a note pad. Bring camcorders for recording video to turn into time capsules and CDs or DVDs with life stories, personal history experiences, memoirs, and events highlighting turning points or special times in people's lives.

STEP 3: Assign each personal historian one or two older persons to interview with the following questions.

1. What were the most significant turning points or events in your life?
2. How did you survive the Wars?

3. What were the highlights, turning points, or significant events that you experienced during the economic downturn of 1929-1939? How did you cope or solve your problems?

4. What did you do to solve your problems during the significant stages of your life at age 10, 20, 30, 40, 50, 60 and 70-plus? Or pick a year that you want to talk about.

5. What changes in your life do you want to remember and pass on to future generations?

6. What was the highlight of your life?

7. How is it best to live your life after 70?

8. What years do you remember most?

9. What was your favorite stage of life?

10. What would you like people to remember about you and the times you lived through?

STEP 3:
Have the student record the older person's answers. Select the most significant events, experiences, or turning points the person chooses to emphasize. Then write the story of that significant event in ten pages or less.

STEP 4: Ask the older person to supply the younger student photos, art work, audio tapes, or video clips. Usually photos, pressed flowers, or art work will be supplied. Have the student or teacher scan the photos onto a disk and return the original photos or art work or music to the owner.

STEP 5:The personal historian, volunteer, student and/or teacher scans the photos and puts them onto a Web site on the Internet at one of the free communities that give away Web site to the public at no cost....some include http://www. tripod.com, http://www.fortunecity.com, http://www.angelfire.com, http://www.geocities.com, and others. Most search engines will give a list of communities at offering free Web sites to the public. Microsoft also offers free family Web sites for family photos and newsletters or information. Ask your Internet service provider whether it offers free Web site space to subscribers. The free Web sites are limited in space.

For larger Web site spaces with room for audio and video material and other keepsake memorabilia, purchase a personal Web site from a Web-hosting company. Shop around for affordable Web site space for a multimedia life story time capsule that would include text, video and/or audio clips, music, art, photos, and any other effects.

1. Create a Web site with text from the older person's significant life events
2. Add photos.
3. Add sound or .wav files with the voice of the older person speaking in small clips or sound bites.
4. Intersperse text and photos or art work with sound, if available.
   Add video clips, if available and won't take too much bandwidth.
5. Put Web site on line as TIME CAPSULE of (insert name of person) interviewed and edited by, insert name of student who interviewed older person.

STEP 6: Label each Web site Time Capsule and collect them in a history archives on the lives of older adults at the turn of the millennium. Make sure the older person and all relatives and friends are emailed the Web site link. You have now created a time capsule for future generations.

This can be used as a classroom exercise in elementary and high schools to teach the following:

1. Making friends with older adults.
2. Learning to write on intergenerational topics.
3. Bringing community together of all generations.
4. Learning about foster grandparents.
5. History lessons from those who lived through history.
6. Learning about diversity and how people of diverse origins lived through the 20th century.
7. Preserving the significant events in the lives of people as time capsules for future generations to know what it was like to live between 1900 and 2000 at any age.
8. Learning to write skits and plays from the life stories of older adults taken down by young students.
9. Teaching older adults skills in creative writing at senior centers.
10. Learning what grandma did during World War 2 or the stock market crash of 1929 followed by the economic downturn of 1930-1938.

What to Ask People about Their Lives before You Write a Play or Skit

Step 1
When you interview, ask for facts and concrete details. Look for statistics, and research whether statistics are deceptive in your case.

Step 2
To write a plan, write one sentence for each topic that moves the story or piece forward. Then summarize for each topic in a paragraph. Use dialogue at least in every third paragraph.

Step 3
Look for the following facts or headings to organize your plan for a biography or life story.

1. PROVERB. Ask the people you interview what would be their proverb or slogan if they had to create/invent a slogan that fit themselves or their aspirations: One slogan might be something like the seventies ad for cigarettes, "We've come a long way, baby," to signify ambition. Only look for an original slogan.

2. PURPOSE. Ask the people you interview or a biography, for what purpose is or was their journey? Is or was it equality in the workplace or something personal and different such as dealing with change—downsizing, working after retirement, or anything else?

3. IMPRINT. Ask what makes an imprint or impact on people's lives and what impact the people you're interviewing want to make on others?

4. STATISTICS: How deceptive are they? How can you use them to focus on reality?

5. How have the people that you're interviewing influenced changes in the way people or corporations function?

6. To what is the person aspiring?

7. What kind of communication skills does the person have and how are these skills received? Are the communication skills male or female, thinking or feeling, yin or yang, soft or steeled, and are people around these people negative or positive about those communication skills?

8. What new styles is the person using? What kind of motivational methods, structure, or leadership? Is the person a follower or leader? How does the person match his or her personality to the character of a corporation or interest?

9. How does the person handle change?
10. How is the person reinforced?

Once you have titles and summarized paragraphs for each segment of your story, you can more easily flesh out the story by adding dialogue and description to your factual information. Look for differences in style between the people you interview? How does the person want to be remembered?

Is the person a risk taker or cautious for survival? Does the person identify with her job or the people involved in the process of doing the work most creatively or originally?

Does creative expression take precedence over processes of getting work out to the right place at the right time? Does the person want his ashes to spell the words "re-invent yourself" where the sea meets the shore? This is a popular concept appearing in various media.

Search the Records in the Family History Library of Salt Lake City, Utah

Make use of the database online at the Family History Library of Salt Lake City, Utah. Or visit the branches in many locations. The Family History Library (FHL) is known worldwide as the focal point of family history records preservation.

The FHL collection contains more than 2.2 million rolls of microfilmed genealogical records, 742,000 microfiche, 300,000 books, and 4,500 periodicals that represent data collected from over 105 countries. You don't have to be a member of any particular church or faith to use the library or to go online and search the records.

Family history records owe a lot to the invention of writing. And then there is oral history, but someone needs to transcribe oral history to record and archive them for the future.

Interestingly, isn't it a coincidence that writing is 6,000 years old and DNA that existed 6,000 years ago first reached such crowded conditions in the very cities that had first used writing extensively to measure accounting and trade had very little recourse but to move on to new areas where there were far less people and less use of writing?

A lot of major turning points occurred 6,000 years ago—the switch to a grain-based diet from a meat and root diet, the use of bread and fermented grain beverages, making of oil from plants, and the rise of religions based on building "god houses" in the centers of town in areas known as the "cereal belt" around the world.

Six thousand years ago in India we have the start of the Sanskrit writings, the cultivation of grain. In China, we have the recording of acupuncture points for medicine built on energy meridians that also show up in the blue tattoos of the Ice Man fossil "Otsi" in the Alps—along the same meridians as the Chinese acupuncture points.

At 6,000 years ago the Indo European languages spread out across Europe. Mass migrations expanded by the Danube leaving pottery along the trade routes that correspond to the clines and gradients of gene frequency coming out of the cereal belts.

Then something happened. There was an agricultural frontier cutting off the agriculturists from the hunters. Isn't it a coincidence that the agricultural frontiers or barriers also are genetic barriers at least to some degree?

Oral History as Monologue or Skit

Here's how to systematically collect, record, and preserve living peoples' testimonies about their own experiences and turn them into plays, skits, or monologues. Record the highlights of significant events in another person's life. With permission and as a team, write a skit or one-act play based on the significant highlights of that person's experience. It can be about what happened during a war or an economic downturn or upturn, or any other event that the person wants you to record and turn into a play, skit, or monologue.

After you record in audio and/or video the highlights of anyone's experiences, try to verify your findings. See whether you can check any facts in order to find out whether the person being recorded is making up the story or whether it really did happen. A one-act play can be fiction or a true life story. You can base your play on a historical character whose life story is not known widely outside of his or her state. Focus on various ethnic groups or dramatize your own favorite ancestor. Choose a historical character that exemplifies a valuable lesson to young actors and audiences. Ask parents what they would most like their children to see in a one-act play. Ask children what makes them laugh.

This is going to be difficult unless you have witnesses or other historical records. Once you have verified your findings to the best of your ability, note whether the findings have been verified. Then analyze what you found. Put the oral history recordings in an accurate historical context.

Mark the recordings with the dates and places. Watch where you store your findings so scholars in the future will be able to access the transcript or recording and convert the recording to another, newer technology. For instance, if you have a transcript on paper, have it saved digitally on a disk and somewhere else on tape and perhaps a written transcript on acid-free good paper in case technology moves ahead before the transcript or recording is converted to the new technology.

For example, if you only put your recording on a phonograph record, within a generation or two, there may not be any phonographs around to play the record. The same goes for CDs, DVDs and audio or video tapes.

So make sure you have a readable paper copy to be transcribed or scanned into the new technology as well as the recordings on disk and tape. For example, if you record someone's experiences in a live interview with your video camera, use a cable to save the video in the hard disk of a computer and then burn the file to a CD or DVD.

Keep a copy of audio tape and a copy of regular video tape—all in a safe place such as a time capsule, and make a copy for various archives in libraries and university oral history preservation centers. Be sure scholars in the future can find a way to enjoy the experiences in your time capsule, scrapbook, or other storage device for oral histories.

Use your DNA testing results to add more information to a historical record. As an interviewer with a video camera and/or audio tape recorder, your task is to record as a historical record what the person who you are interviewing recollects.

The events move from the person being interviewed to you, the interviewer, and then into various historical records. In this way you can combine results of DNA testing with actual memories of events. If it's possible, also take notes or have someone take notes in case the tape doesn't pick up sounds clearly.

I had the experience of having a video camera battery go out in spite of all precautions when I was interviewing someone, and only the audio worked. So keep a backup battery on hand whether you use a tape recorder or a video camera. If at all possible, have a partner bring a spare camera and newly recharged battery. A fully charged battery left overnight has a good chance of going out when you need it.

Emphasize Simplicity in Plays

Emphasize the *commitment* to family and faith. Love in teenage drama is defined as commitment to helping others reach their potential. To create readers' and media attention to an oral history, it should have some redemptive value to a universal audience. That's the most important point. Make your oral history simple and earthy. Write about real people who have values, morals, and a faith in something greater than themselves that is equally valuable to readers or viewers.

Publishers who buy an oral history written as a book on its buzz (public relations) value are buying *simplicity*. It is simplicity that sells and nothing else but simplicity. This is true for oral histories, instructional materials, and fiction. It's good storytelling to say it simply.

Simplicity means the oral history or memoirs book or story gives you all the answers you were looking for in your life in exotic places, but found it close by. What's the great proverb that your oral history is telling the world?

Is it to stand on your own two feet and put bread on your own table for your family? That's the moral point, to pull your own weight, and pulling your own weight is a buzz word that sells oral histories and fiction that won't preach, but instead teach and reach through simplicity.

That's the backbone of the oral historian's new media. Buzz means the story is simple to understand. You make the complex easier to grasp. And buzz means you can sell your story or book, script or narrative by focusing on the values of simplicity, morals, faith, and universal values that hold true for everyone.

Doing the best to take care of your family sells and is buzz appeal, hot stuff in the publishing market of today and in the oral history archives. This is true, regardless of genre. Publishers go through fads every two years—angel books, managing techniques books, computer home-based business books, novels about ancient historical characters or tribes, science fiction, children's programming, biography, and oral history transcribed into a book or play.

The genres shift emphasis, but values are consistent in the bestselling books. Perhaps your oral history will be simple enough to become a bestselling book or script. In the new media, simplicity is buzz along with values.

Oral history, like best-selling novels and true stories is built on simplicity, values, morals, and commitment. Include how one person dealt with about trends. Focus your own oral history about life in the lane of your choice. Develop one central issue and divide that issue into a few important questions that highlight or focus on that one central issue.

When you write or speak a personal history either alone or in an interview, you focus on determining the order of your life story. Don't use flashbacks. Focus on the highlights and turning points. Organize what you'll say or write. An autobiography deals in people's relationships. Your autobiography deals as much with what doesn't change—the essentials—as what life changes you and those around you go through.

Your autobiography should be more concrete than abstract. You want the majority of people to understand what you mean. Say what you mean, and mean what you say. More people understand concrete details than understand abstract ideas.

Be personal in a life story. The more personal you are, the more eternal is your life story. More people will view or read it again and again far into the future. You can emphasize your life's journey and look at the world through your own eyes. To make the structure salable, 'meander' your life as you would travel on a journey. Perhaps you're a winding river meandering around obstacles and competitors. At each stop, you learn your own capabilities and your own place in the world.

The more you meander, the more you take away the urgency from your story that sets up tension in the audience and keeps them on the edge of their seat. Don't let the meandering overpower your sense of urgency. Don't dwell on your reaction. Focus on your action to people and situations. Stay active in your own personal history. In other words, don't repeat how you reacted, but show how you acted.

Before you sit down to write your autobiography, think of yourself in terms of going on a journey inside the privacy of your purse or wallet. May your purse is the only place where you really do have any privacy. Come up for air when you have hit bottom. Bob up to the sunshine, completely changed or at least matured.

If you have really grown, you will not be blinded by the light, in the figurative sense, as the song goes. Instead, the light gives you insight. So now you have vision along with some hindsight. The next step is learning how to promote and market your salable personal history or life story.

A biography reports the selected events of another person's life—usually 12 major events in the six various significant events also known as "turning points" and also known as "transition points" of life that would include the highlights of significant events for each of the six stages of growth: 1) infanthood, 2) childhood, 3) teen years 4) young adulthood 5)middle life 6)maturity.

Chapter Eight

Life Story Plays as Dialogues with the Higher Self

If your autobiography has punch and power, is marketable and makes viewers want to network and discuss it in quality circles, you life story will make a concrete impact on the abstract idea of diary writing. Some pause to write from introspection and reflection. Others prefer to write action from biography. Your mission, should you decide to broadcast it, is to locate business people who want to buy or sell a true life story. It's as profitable for them as it's a healing experience for you if you see it as an exercise in getting to know yourself. Writing and recording your personal history is a search for your core identity.

Personal history writing and speaking or recording reminds me of Stan Dale's quote, "Intimacy is spelled "in to me you see." The quote also is listed on the *New Intimacy* Web site at http://www.menstuff.org/columns/newintimacy/52.html.

Writing personal history is writing about intimacy. An autobiography helps you practice seeing another person with your soul. Writing the life story as a play, skit, or monologue for high-school performers or older adults offers you a vitality. In the writing process, you see who you are and make a connection with others who shaped your world as you, in turn, shaped the world of those around you.

When you write your autobiography, listen with your body. One of the conclusions many autobiography writers arrive at is "I am never enough." This decision isn't commercial, although the story line with an upbeat ending is marketable. The "not enough" feeling you write in your diary creates fear and loneliness.

What would happen if you took a plot line of a protagonist who says: "I'm not enough or give me a break" and linked it with an antagonist who says: "I need a connection." You have opposites, perhaps a couple. One says, "I need a break." The other replies, "Not until I have a connection."

Then your power-punch your one-liner in the dialogue. "Give me a break" could mask profound loneliness with a tough outer shell (as in I don't need anybody). Your antagonist might continue with a response that repeated "Not without a connection."

The dialogue would be between two people who want a relationship so eagerly that one of them could be more willing to openly work lovingly for it. Your premise would be that the protagonist is really saying, "I don't know how to connect."

The audience sees the deep suffering and the false armor in dialogue and visual action. Not everyone wants other people in a personal history. Do you really want you and your competition in your personal history video? Not unless you're making a feature film about your life.

In reality, you can sell your life story to a small press publisher, to an independent, low-budget producer, or produce it as a play for a few thousand dollars in a local theatre. What else can you expect? That all depends on how commercial your story is written in the eyes of the big studios.

The least expensive way to handle a personal history is to put it on a DVD and on a CD. Have a text copy, and if you have a Web site, upload the video clip and text to the Web as a time capsule. Designate someone to take over the payments on the Web site when you can no longer maintain it. You can even rent an option to someone else's life story's movie rights.

If you want power over your life story, look at the structure of your personal history. If you know you have a salable story, how many ways can you market your autobiographical or biographical writing?

One way to market your story is by utilizing interactive computer software to help yourself and others to write their own life events document. There are several computer software disks on the market that will organize your life story events.

You can form quality circles and teach life story writing to groups, including adult education classes and at senior community centers. Plays are in demand for children, junior high, high school, and college-age performers and audiences as well as performers and audiences of mature adults/senior citizens at their community centers and lifelong learning programs.

Will Computer Software Help You Write Your Life Story?

You may first wish to market your autobiography on computer software disks. Interactive fiction is a writing game recorded on a computer floppy disk which allows the player to answer questions, but the easiest way is to put your video on a DVD.

There are alternative answers. This game is suitable for playing "What if I chose the road not taken? What would my life story be like, then?" To create and market an interactive fiction autobiography game, hire an independent programmer who specializes in programming floppy disk software with questions and alternative answers.

Turn a keepsake album into a skit for a time capsule. Put your life story on the Web or on a DVD and CD at the same time you publish it as a book. Self-publishing will give you the electronic and audio rights to your book. With print-on-demand publishing, you lose your electronic rights in many cases. Check out your contract.

If you go the way of complicated interactive story writing, you'll need to work with someone who knows how to create interactive stories. When a player is interactive, it means he/she interacts with the computer in a learning situation.

For example, the computer software could be designed to ask you these following questions: "What if you chose to become a paralegal instead of a full-time freelance writer? Would freelance writers have the starving artist mentality? What if your fiction always has been rejected? What if you are totally dependent on relatives for support? Where would you be working today?

Would you be happy? How much would you be earning? Who would you meet and marry? Would he/she be kind or abusive? Would you be a co-dependent seeking to be parented?

Interactive software allows you to play the possibilities or create new realities in the present. You can team up with a programmer. Another alternative is using strictly autobiographical software to organize your life story like a diary. You can look back on the result and judge whether it is commercial or strictly for the family genealogy collection.

You may wish to use software to organize your own life story and print out a document. Some story organizing software breaks your history into manageable sections. In fact, some story writing software offer more than 400 specific questions to prompt you to provide details of each area of your life. If you use this type of software, you answer by keyboarding in all the important details into your computer. Then you save it on a disk for posterity. Answer only the questions you choose.

The programs work by advancing one screen at a time when you feel like it. You can spend years writing your autobiography or just a few days. The programs include topics such as your birth, medical events, friends, education, property, holidays, achievements, and other categories. These types of story writing programs might organize various categories and the facts in them so you can glance at your life and decide whether to turn it into a novel, a screenplay, a stage play, video, radio play, audio, or leave it as a book for the family eyes only.

When you're finished typing in the details of each event, you can print your story or export the file to your word processing program or desktop publishing software for formatting into a small tale or a full document. Some of these programs allow you to write a large number of pages, even up to 3,000 pages.

You can print out the document and have it bound in a cover by a photocopying company. Then present it to each family member as a holiday gift. You can use this document to set the record straight, to write your memoirs, or to create every detail of your life or any one else's life for relatives or for history.

Long after you're gone, your descendants will read it. You can even explain why you included or excluded certain relatives out of your will.

You can pass on information about your marriage to your children so they would repeat or avoid the same choices based on the events of your early childhood programming or whatever you choose to detail. Public domain software offers various programs on creating diaries and life events on software. For other types of software consult software catalogues, public domain software listings, computer bulletin boards and trade journals.

Software can be used two ways: 1: To sell your own autobiography interactive games or 2: To organize and print out your own life events by answering interactive questions on already existing autobiography-writing software. Desktop video combines computer software, burning files to DVD and/or CDs, and transferring videotape played on your VCR to DVD disks. Sometimes desktop publishing combines with desktop video also known as multimedia authoring.

You may choose to create video programs that can be used interactively with computer software to ask someone hundreds of questions about autobiographical events. I like putting material on CDs or DVDs and mailing them to my online students when I used to teach university-level writing and speaking courses entirely online.

If you're a facilitator, you can help others to write, illustrate or to express themselves in multimedia. Writing personal histories interactively with video and computers works very well with senior citizens taking an autobiography writing class in a community center.

Psychotherapists will also find this introspective way of writing works well with clients who would rather share their innermost thoughts and details of life events with a computer. To protect the privacy of people, it's a good way of "getting thoughts and feelings off your chest in words.

When you go public, ask yourself how your researched information can be of help to others who seek your information for making choices and decisions in their own lives. Personal history writing also helps you seek self-identity and share your introspective feelings on paper or through interviews on video or audio without direct contact with a group. You can dialogue with the questions on the computer in total privacy.

Chapter Nine

Selling Life Stories as One-Act Plays, Skits, or Monologues

Launch your salable life story in the major national press and in various newspapers and magazines of niche markets related to the events in your life, such as weekly newspapers catering to a group: senior citizens, your ethnic group, your local area, or your occupation or area of interest. Your personal history time capsule may be saved to disk and also uploaded to the Web. What about looking for movie deals and book publishers?

If you don't have the money to produce your autobiography as a video biography, or even a film or commercial movie, or publish it for far less cost as a print-on-demand published book, you may wish to find a co-production partner to finance the production of your life story as a cinematic film or made-for-TV video.

At the same time you could contact literary agents and publishers, but one front-page article in a national newspaper or daily newspaper can do wonders to move your life story in front of the gaze of publishers and producers. While you're waiting for a reporter to pay attention to the news angle you have selected for your life story, I highly recommend Michael Wiese's book <u>Film and Video Marketing</u> because it lists some co-production partners as the following:

Private Investors/Consortiums

Foreign Governments (blocked funds)

Financiers

Corporations

Theatrical Distributors

International Theatrical Distributors

International Sales Agents

Home Video

International Home Video

Pay TV

Syndicators

Record Companies

Music Publishers

Book Publishers

Toy Companies

Licensing and Merchandising Firms

Sponsors (products, services)

Public Relations Firms

Marketing Companies/Consultants

Film Bookers

You can also contact actors, directors, producers, feature distributors, home video distributors, entertainment lawyers, brokers, accountants, animation houses, production houses, video post production houses, labs, film facilities, and agents with your script and ask the owners whether they'd be interested in bartering budget items, deferring, or investing in your script. Private investors could also be professional investors, venture capitalists, and even doctors and dentists who may wish to finance a movie if the potential interests them. You can sell points in your film to investors who finance it as a group of investors, each buying a small percentage of the film for an investment fee.

Or you can approach film investment corporations that specialize in investing in and producing films as partners. They are publicized or listed in the entertainment trade magazines going to producers and workers in the entertainment and film or video industry.

You market your script not only to agents and producers, but to feature distributors, film financiers and co-production partners. This is the first step in finding a way to take your autobiography from script to screen. Learn who distributes what before you approach anyone.

If you want to approach video instead of film, you might wish to know that children's video programming is the fastest-growing genre in original programming. Children's titles account for 10%-15% of the overall home video revenues. According to one of Michael Wiese's books written in the nineties, *Home Video: Producing For The Home Market,* "With retail prices falling and alternative retail outlets expanding, children's programming will soon become one of the most profitable segments of the video market." He was right. What has happened in the new millennium is that children's program is doing wonderfully. Why? Children's video is repeatable. Children watch the same tape 30 to 50 times. Children's video sells for comparatively lower prices than feature films.

Children's video also rents well. Children's tapes sell it toy stores, book stores, children's stores, and in stores like Woolworth's and Child World. Manufacturers sell tapes at Toy Fair and the American Booksellers Association conventions.

For these reasons, you may wish to write your autobiography as a script for children's video or as a children's book. Video is a burgeoning industry.

According to the market research firm, Fairfield Group, in 1985, the prerecorded video business earned $ 3.3 billion in sales and rentals. This nearly equaled the record and theatrical box office revenues for the same year. The world VCR population is about 100 million. Today we have the DVD and the Internet streaming video.

Back in 1985, the U.S. and Japan accounted for half of the VCRs, followed by the United Kingdom, (9 million) West Germany (nearly 7 million), and Canada, Australia, Turkey, and France (about 3 million each). Spain reported 2 million VCRs. By 1991, the number of VCR ownership increased as prices slowly came down.

Today, in the 21st century, the prerecorded video business has quickly moved to DVD disks, downloadable at a price Internet-based movies, and video tapes are on the way to being a memory of the eighties and early nineties. In the next decade, another media format will be in fashion to replace videos on DVDs and streaming Internet video. The idea is to keep transferring the story from one form of technology to another so that videos made today will be able to be viewed by people in the next century.

The European VCR markets grew faster than in the U.S. during the eighties and nineties just as the DVD markets grew in the early 21st century because there were fewer entertainment alternatives—fewer TV stations, restricted viewing hours, fewer pay TV services, and fewer movie theatres.

You should not overlook the foreign producers for your script. Include Canadian cable T.V., foreign agents, and foreign feature film and video producers among your contacts. Most university libraries open to the public for research include directories listing foreign producers. Photocopy their addresses and send them a query letter and one-page synopsis of your script. Don't overlook the producers from non-English speaking countries. Your script can be translated or dubbed.

You might attend film market type conventions and conferences. They draw producers from a variety of countries. In 1989 at the former Cinetex Film Market in Las Vegas, producers from Canada, Italy, Israel, Spain, and other foreign countries sat next to script writers. All of them were receptive to receiving scripts. They handed one another their business cards. You can learn a lot at summer film markets and film festivals about what kind of scripts are in demand.

Keep a list of which film markets will meet. In the U.S. there are 3 to 5 film markets a year and many more film festivals. Seek out the foreign and local producers with track records and see whether they'd be interested in your script if you have a life story in the form of a script, treatment, or story. Perhaps your theme has some relation to a producer's country or ethnic group. Lots of films are made in Asia, in the Middle East (Israel, Egypt and Tunisia), in Latin America, and Europe or Canada.

Seek out the Australian producers also and New Zealand or India. If you have a low-budget film or home video script set in Korea, Philippines, Japan, or Taiwan, or a specialty film such as Karate or something that appeals to the Indian film market, contact those producers and script agents in those countries. Find out the budget limitations that producers have in the different countries.

Social issues documentaries based on your autobiography are another market for home video. Vestron and other home video distributors use hard-hitting documentaries. Collecting documentary video tapes is like collecting copies of <u>National Geographic</u> magzine. You never throw them out. Tapes are also sold by direct mail. Companies producing and distributing documentaries include MCA, MGM/UA, Vestron, Victory, CBS/Fox, Warner, Media, Karl, Monterey, Thorn/EMI, Embassy, and USA, to name a few.

If you write your autobiography or another's biography as a romance, you might wish to write a script for the video romance series market. Romance video has its roots in the paperback novel. However, the biggest publishers of romance novels have little recognition in retail video stores.

Among consumers, yes; wholesalers and retailers, no. Bookstores, yes. The problem is with pricing. To sell romance videos in bookstores, the tapes would have to be sold at less than $29. In video stores, they can be positioned the same as $59 feature films on video.

Production costs to make high quality romance videos are high. Top stars, top writers, hit book titles, exotic locations, music and special effects are required.

Huge volumes of tapes must be sold to break even. Then producers have to search for pay TV, broadcast, or foreign partners. The budget for a one-hour video tape of a thin romance story comes to $500,000.

It's far better to make a low-budget feature film. Romance as a genre has never previously appealed to the video retail buyer. In contrast, a romance paperback sells for a few dollars. Now the question remains: Would women buy a romance-genre video DVD priced at $9.95?

Romance novels successfully have been adapted to audio tape for listening at far less than the cost of video. There is a market for audio scripts of short romance novels and novellas. What is becoming popular today are videos and 'movies' downloadable from the Internet that you can watch on your computer screen or save to a DVD since DVD burners became affordable and popular. Try adapting highlights of your romance or life story novel to a play, skit, or monologue.

The only way romance videos would work is by putting together a multi-partnered structure that combines pay TV, home video, book publishing, and domestic and foreign TV. In the eighties, was anyone doing romance video tapes? Yes. Prism Video produced six feature-length romance films, acquired from Comworld. In 1985 the tapes sold for $11.95.

Comworld had limited TV syndication exposure and was one of the first to come out with romance videos. Karl/Lorimar came out with eight romance films from L/A House Productions on a budget of $400,000 each. They were also priced at $11.95 in 1985. To break even, a company has to sell about 60,000 units per title.

Twenty years later, think about adapting to a play the romance DVD video and the downloadable Internet video. What's available to adapt as educational material? Write for various age groups on niche subjects that would appeal to teachers. Follow their rules on what is appropriate for their classrooms. The market also is open for stage and radio/Internet broadcast skits and plays geared to older adults as performers and audiences.

Other media are like open doors to finding a way to put your life story on a disk. Any interview, script, or story can go from print-on-demand published novel or true story book to radio script or stage play. A video can move from a digital high 8 camcorder with a Firewire 1394 cable attached to a personal computer rapidly into the hard disk drive via Windows XP Movie Maker software. From there it can be saved as a WMV file (a Windows Media file). Then the file can be recorded on a DVD, if long, or a CD if under one hour. Poems can be written, read, and 'burned' to a compact disk (CD) and then mailed out as greeting cards, love letters, or personal histories. Short videos can be emailed.

Romance or life story highlights novels and scripts on audio tape cost less to produce. This market occasionally advertises for romantic novel manuscripts,

scripts, and stories in a variety of writer's magazines. Check out the needs of various magazines for journalists and writers online. If you read a lot of romance genre novels or write in this style, you may want to write your autobiography in this genre, but you'd have to market to publishers who use this genre or biographies in other genres such as factual biography.

If your autobiography is set on events which occurred in your childhood, you might prefer to concentrate on writing appropriate for children's video programming. It's a lot easier to sell to the producers who are basking in the current explosion of children's video programming. Perhaps it's your mission to use the video format to teach children.

Will the script of your life story do the following?

teach,

mentor,

motivate,

inspire,

or inform viewers who can be:

children,

teenagers,

parents

or midlifers on their quests for self-identify:

or in their search for facts:

to use as guidelines in making their own decisions:

about life's journeys and writing an introspective journal?

Can your diary be dynamic, dramatic, and empowering to others who may be going through similar stages of life? Are your characters charismatic and memorable, likable and strong?

A life story or autobiography when videotaped or filed as a feature-length movie can spring out of a diary or an inner personal journal (which dialogues with the people who impact your life and observes selected, important events).

Chapter Ten

Adapting Current Events or History

Writing Plays, Skits, or Monologues from Current Events or History:

Diaries, like deleted files hidden in the cache pits of computers, and DNA tests can be used as evidence. Diaries also hold the seeds of a story. You could write a novel or a screenplay from a diary. A diary also is a history.

Preserve a diary as you would restore and preserve a valuable work of art from the past. Diaries are meant to be passed to future generations for a glimpse into a world that can be experienced by generations far into the future. Keep a file of dates listed in the diary and any objects that surrounded the diary from the same era.

A story with a central issue needed little explanation when one woman wrote in her diary in the style of a telegram: "October 25, 1926: First day of honeymoon. On train to Miami. Today I died." What central issues and themes tell a story in the diaries that cross your path? Instead of writing about pain, write to cheer people up with nourishment. That's why nourishment-for-the-soul-themed books are popular. People want to be cheered up, not always read your painful experiences. Write so people will feel important about themselves, feel good, positive, and nourished from how you solved your problems or gained results. Write about current events, social history and issues, or real life experiences that transformed you. People read or watch a play also for information they can use in making decisions and choices.

It's not always escape or distraction from real life, but nourishment and solutions to problems that offer action, closure, and hope. Plays that offer harmony and serenity as escape and distraction also form part of the plays and skits of nourishment skits. Don't always give them pain to read. It's therapeutic for you, but not as a steady diet for your audiences.

They already watch the news on TV. How can you transcend and transform the news as nourishment and reality, and still sell escape? Keep the dates and topics organized if you are working with restoring and preserving diaries and turning them into skits and plays for various age groups. There should be a central issue or theme. How old was the person writing the diary? How many years did the individual keep the diary? What kind of objects were near the diary, packed together?

What kind of dust or other stains were on the diary—sawdust? Farm materials and plants? The first corsage from the senior prom? How about recipes, household hints, or how-to tips for hobbies? Was the diary or journal personal and inner-reflected, or geared toward outer events in the world? Were anecdotes about people and/or pets included, or was it about the feelings of the author of the diary?

Find out what other clues the mystery of the diary unfolds, from the lipstick or nail polish stain to the sawdust and coffee stains, or that faint smell of tobacco, industrial lint, or is it lavender, jasmine or farm dust and straw? Look inside the box in which the diary was packed. It's all evidence and clues waiting to be examined just like a mystery novel. A diary is a story, and everyone life deserves a novel, story, or biography and eventually, a place in a time capsule.

Chapter Eleven

Restoring Diaries to be Turned into Plays, Monologues, or Skits

Make a book jacket for your diary to preserve and restore it. Use acid-free paper. Call a library or museum and ask for a brand or type of long-lasting acid-free paper and where you can buy some. Put a title and label on the dust jacket with the name of the diary's author and any dates, city, state, or country.

You can also speak to the art history department of most universities and find out what kind of paper is best to use for a book jacket to restore and preserve a diary. Treat it like a work of art. The same can be done for photo scrap books.

If torn, mend the diary. Your goal is to improve its condition. Apply a protective plastic wrapper to your valuable dust jacket. Give the diary a dust jacket in good condition. It should start to look more like a valuable book in good condition. If the diary is dingy and dirty, bleach it white on the edges. Put a plastic cover on the diary. The white pages of a diary without ink can be bleached with regular household bleach, but don't let the vapors of the bleach soak through to reach the ink because it will bleach out the writing.

Repair old diaries and turn them into heirlooms for families and valuable collectibles. The current price for repair of handwritten diaries and books is about $35 and up per book or bound diary, if you like to specialize in mending old dairies and family or personal books for a fee.

Some old diaries contain recipes and also served as personal, handwritten cookbooks containing recipes created by a particular family or family cook. These were valuable books preserved as if they were family scrapbooks, unlike the recipe databases in computers we have today. They are works of art, like an old tapestry embroidered with the story of a family's major turning points and events. For more repair tips on bound diaries and books, I recommend *How to Wrap a Book*, Fannie Merit Farmer, Boston Cooking School.

How do you repair an old diary to make it more valuable to the heirs? You'll often find a bound diary that's torn in the seams. According to Barbara Gelink, of the Collector's Old Cookbooks Club, San Diego, whom I interviewed in the 1990s for a magazine article, to repair a book, you take a bottle of Book Saver Glue (or any other book-repairing or wood glue), and spread the glue along the binder.

Run the glue along the seam and edges. Use wax paper to keep the glue from getting where it shouldn't. Put a heavy glass bottle on the inside page to hold it down while the glue dries.

To remove tape, tags, or stains from a glossy cover, use lighter fluid or cleaning fluid (away from sparks, flames, or heat lamps). Dampen a cloth with nail polish remover if lighter fluid is too smelly and flammable for you.

Another way to remove something pasted on a plastic book cover is to use the finest grade sandpaper. Many books you'll find at goodwill will have adhesive price tags on the book. It's not usual to find diaries, even bound diaries in old book stores, but they show up in garage sales and in some antique stores and flea markets along with old photos.

Chapter Twelve

Interviewing Techniques for Videobiographies

Interview and Camcorder Techniques for Recording Life Stories and Highlights You'll Write as Plays, Dramatizations, or Skits

The events move from the person being interviewed to you, the interviewer, and then into various historical records. In this way you can combine results of DNA testing with actual memories of events. If it's possible, also take notes or have someone take notes in case the tape doesn't pick up sounds clearly.

Keep a backup battery on hand whether you use a tape recorder or a video camera. If at all possible, have a partner bring a spare camera and newly recharged battery. A fully charged battery left overnight has a good chance of going out when you need it.

What Should Go Into a Life Story Play, Skit, or Dramatization?

Emphasize the commitment to family and faith. To create readers' and media attention to an oral history, it should have some redemptive value to a universal audience. That's the most important point. Make your oral history simple and earthy. Write about real people who have values, morals, and a faith in something greater than themselves that is equally valuable to readers or viewers.

Publishers who buy an oral history written as a book on its buzz value are buying simplicity. It is simplicity that sells and nothing else but simplicity. This is true for oral histories, instructional materials, and fiction. It's good storytelling to say it simply.

Simplicity means the oral history or memoirs book or story gives you all the answers you were looking for in your life in exotic places, but found it close by. What's the great proverb that your oral history is telling the world?

Is it to stand on your own two feet and put bread on your own table for your family? That's the moral point, to pull your own weight, and pulling your own weight is a buzz word that sells oral histories and fiction that won't preach, but instead teach and reach through simplicity.

That's the backbone of the oral historian's new media. Buzz means the story is simple to understand. You make the complex easier to grasp. And buzz means you can sell your story or book, script or narrative by focusing on the values of simplicity, morals, faith, and universal values that hold true for everyone.

Doing the best to take care of your family sells and is buzz appeal, hot stuff in the publishing market of today and in the oral history archives. This is true, regardless of genre. Publishers go through fads every two years—angel books, managing techniques books, computer home-based business books, novels about ancient historical characters or tribes, science fiction, children's programming, biography, and oral history transcribed into a book or play.

The genres shift emphasis, but values are consistent in the bestselling books. Perhaps your oral history will be simple enough to become a bestselling book or script. In the new media, simplicity is buzz along with values. Oral history, like best-selling novels and true stories is built on simplicity, values, morals, and commitment. Include how one person dealt with about trends. Focus your own oral history about life in the lane of your choice.

Chapter Thirteen

Steps to Take in Gathering Life Story Highlights to Write into Plays or Skits

Use the following sequence when gathering oral/aural histories:

1. Develop one central issue and divide that issue into a few important questions that highlight or focus on that one central issue.
2. Write out a plan just like a business plan for your oral history project. You may have to use that plan later to ask for a grant for funding, if required. Make a list of all your products that will result from the oral history when it's done.
3. Write out a plan for publicity or public relations and media relations. How are you going to get the message to the public or special audiences?
4. Develop a budget. This is important if you want a grant or to see how much you'll have to spend on creating an oral history project.
5. List the cost of video taping and editing, packaging, publicity, and help with audio or special effects and stock shot photos of required.
6. What kind of equipment will you need? List that and the time slots you give to each part of the project. How much time is available? What are your deadlines?
7. What's your plan for a research? How are you going to approach the people to get the interviews? What questions will you ask?

8. Do the interviews. Arrive prepared with a list of questions. It's okay to ask the people the kind of questions they would like to be asked. Know what dates the interviews will cover in terms of time. Are you covering the economic depression of the thirties? World Wars? Fifties? Sixties? Pick the time parameters.

9. Edit the interviews so you get the highlights of experiences and events, the important parts. Make sure what's important to you also is important to the person you interviewed.

10. Find out what the interviewee wants to emphasize perhaps to highlight events in a life story. Create a video-biography of the highlights of one person's life or an oral history of an event or series of events.

11. Process audio as well as video, and make sure you have written transcripts of anything on audio and/or video in case the technology changes or the tapes go bad.

12. Save the tapes to compact disks, DVDs, a computer hard disk and several other ways to preserve your oral history time capsule. Donate any tapes or CDs to appropriate archives, museums, relatives of the interviewee, and one or more oral history libraries. They are usually found at universities that have an oral history department and library such as UC Berkeley and others.

13. Check the Web for oral history libraries at universities in various states and abroad.

14. Evaluate what you have edited. Make sure the central issue and central questions have been covered in the interview. Find out whether newspapers or magazines want summarized transcripts of the audio and/or video with photos.

15. Contact libraries, archives, university oral history departments and relevant associations and various ethnic genealogy societies that focus on the subject matter of your central topic.

16. Keep organizing what you have until you have long and short versions of your oral history for various archives and publications. Contact magazines and newspapers to see whether editors would assign reporters to do a story on the oral history project.

17. Create a scrapbook with photos and summarized oral histories. Write a synopsis of each oral history on a central topic or issue. Have speakers give public presentations of what you have for each person interviewed and/or for the entire project using highlights of several interviews with the media for publicity. Be sure your project is archived properly and stored in a place devoted to oral history archives and available to researchers and authors.

Aural/Oral History Techniques

1. Begin with easy to answer questions that don't require you explore and probe deeply in your first question. Focus on one central issue when asking questions. Don't use abstract questions. A plain question would be "What's your purpose?" An abstract question with connotations would be "What's your crusade?" Use questions with denotations instead of connotations. Keep questions short and plain—easy to understand. Examples would be, "What did you want to accomplish? How did you solve those problems? How did you find closure?" Ask the familiar "what, when, who, where, how, and why."

2. First research written or visual resources before you begin to seek an oral history of a central issue, experience, or event.

3. Who is your intended audience?

4. What kind of population niche or sample will you target?

5. What means will you select to choose who you will interview? What group of people will be central to your interview?

6. Write down how you'll explain your project. Have a script ready so you don't digress or forget what to say on your feet.

7. Consult oral history professionals if you need more information. Make sure what you write in your script will be clear to understand by your intended audience.

8. Have all the equipment you need ready and keep a list of what you'll use and the cost. Work up your budget.

9. Choose what kind of recording device is best—video, audio, multimedia, photos, and text transcript. Make sure your video is broadcast quality. I use a Sony Digital eight (high eight) camera.

10. Make sure from cable TV stations or news stations that what type of video and audio you choose ahead of time is broadcast quality.

11. Make sure you have an external microphone and also a second microphone as a second person also tapes the interview in case the quality of your camera breaks down. You can also keep a tape recorder going to capture the audio in case your battery dies.

12. Make sure your battery is fully charged right before the interview. Many batteries die down after a day or two of nonuse.

13. Test all equipment before the interview and before you leave your office or home. I've had batteries go down unexpectedly and happy there was another person ready with another video camera waiting and also an audio tape version going.

14. Make sure the equipment works if it's raining, hot, cold, or other weather variations. Test it before the interview. Practice interviewing someone on your equipment several times to get the hang of it before you show up at the interview.

15. Make up your mind how long the interview will go before a break and use tape of that length, so you have one tape for each segment of the interview. Make several copies of your interview questions.

16. Be sure the interviewee has a copy of the questions long before the interview so the person can practice answering the questions and think of what to say or even take notes. Keep checking your list of what you need to do.

17. Let the interviewee make up his own questions if he wants. Perhaps your questions miss the point. Present your questions first. Then let him embellish the questions or change them as he wants to fit the central issue with his own experiences.

18. Call the person two days and then one day before the interview to make sure the individual will be there on time and understands how to travel to the location. Or if you are going to the person's home, make sure you understand how to get there.

19. Allow yourself one extra hour in case of traffic jams.

20. Choose a quiet place. Turn off cell phones and any ringing noises. Make sure you are away from barking dogs, street noise, and other distractions.

21. Before you interview make sure the person knows he or she is going to be video and audio-taped.

22. If you don't want anyone swearing, make that clear it's for public archives and perhaps broadcast to families.

23. Your interview questions should follow the journalist's information-seeking format of asking, who, what, where, where, how, and why. Oral history is a branch of journalistic research.

24. Let the person talk and don't interrupt. You be the listener and think of oral history as aural history from your perspective.

25. Make sure only one person speaks without being interrupted before someone else takes his turn to speak.

26. Understand silent pauses are for thinking of what to say.

27. Ask one question and let the person gather his thoughts.

28. Finish all your research on one question before jumping to the next question. Keep it organized by not jumping back to the first question after the second is done. Stay in a linear format.

29. Follow up what you can about any one question, finish with it, and move on to the next question without circling back. Focus on listening instead of asking rapid fire questions as they would confuse the speaker.

30. Ask questions that allow the speaker to begin to give a story, anecdote, life experience, or opinion along with facts. Don't ask questions that can be answered only be yes or no. This is not a courtroom. Let the speaker elaborate with facts and feelings or thoughts.

31. Late in the interview, start to ask questions that explore and probe for deeper answers.

32. Wrap up with how the person solved the problem, achieved results, reached a conclusion, or developed an attitude, or found the answer. Keep the wrap-up on a light, uplifting note.

33. Don't leave the individual hanging in emotion after any intensity of. Respect the feelings and opinions of the person. He or she may see the situation from a different point of view than someone else. So respect the person's right to feel as he does. Respect his need to recollect his own experiences.

34. Interview for only one hour at a time. If you have only one chance, interview for an hour. Take a few minutes break. Then interview for the second hour. Don't interview more than two hours at any one meeting.

35. Use prompts such as paintings, photos, music, video, diaries, vintage clothing, crafts, antiques, or memorabilia when appropriate. Carry the photos in labeled files or envelopes to show at appropriate times in order to prime the memory of the interviewee. For example, you may show a childhood photo and ask "What was it like in that orphanage where these pictures were taken?" Or travel photos might suggest a trip to America as a child, or whatever the photo suggests. For example, "Do you remember when this ice cream parlor inside the ABC movie house stood at the corner of X and Y Street? Did you go there as a teenager? What was your funniest memory of this movie theater or the ice cream store inside back in the fifties?"

36. As soon as the interview is over, label all the tapes and put the numbers in order.

37. A signed release form is required before you can broadcast anything. So have the interviewee sign a release form before the interview.

38. Make sure the interviewee gets a copy of the tape and a transcript of what he or she said on tape. If the person insists on making corrections, send the paper transcript of the tape for correction to the interviewee. Edit the tape as best you can or have it edited professionally.

39. Make sure you comply with all the corrections the interviewee wants changed. He or she may have given inaccurate facts that need to be corrected on the paper transcript.

40. Have the tape edited with the corrections, even if you have to make a tape at the end of the interviewee putting in the corrections that couldn't be edited out or changed.

41. As a last resort, have the interviewee redo the part of the tape that needs correction and have it edited in the tape at the correct place marked on the tape. Keep the paper transcript accurate and up to date, signed with a release form by the interviewee.

42. Oral historians write a journal of field notes about each interview. Make sure these get saved and archived so they can be read with the transcript.

43. Have the field notes go into a computer where someone can read them along with the transcript of the oral history tape or CD.

44. Thank the interviewee in writing for taking the time to do an interview for broadcast and transcript.

45. Put a label on everything you do from the interview to the field notes. Make a file and sub file folders and have everything stored in a computer, in archived storage, and in paper transcript.

46. Make copies and digital copies of all photos and put into the records in a computer. Return originals to owners.

47. Make sure you keep your fingerprints off the photos by wearing white cotton gloves. Use cardboard when sending the photos back and pack securely. Also photocopy the photos and scan the photos into your computer. Treat photos as antique art history in preservation.

48. Make copies for yourself of all photos, tapes, and transcripts. Use your duplicates, and store the original as the master tape in a place that won't be used often, such as a time capsule or safe, or return to a library or museum where the original belongs.

49. Return all original photos to the owners. An oral history archive library or museum also is suitable for original tapes. Use copies only to work from, copy, or distribute.

50. Index your tapes and transcripts. To use oral history library and museum terminology, recordings and transcripts are given "accession numbers."

51. Phone a librarian in an oral history library of a university for directions on how to assign accession numbers to your tapes and transcripts if the materials are going to be stored at that particular library. Store copies in separate places in case of loss or damage.

52. If you don't know where the materials will be stored, use generic accession numbers to label your tapes and transcripts. Always keep copies available for yourself in case you have to duplicate the tapes to send to an institution, museum, or library, or to a broadcast company.

53. Make synopses available to public broadcasting radio and TV stations.

54. Check your facts.

55. Are you missing anything you want to include?

56. Is there some place you want to send these tapes and transcripts such as an ethnic museum, radio show, or TV satellite station specializing in the topics on the tapes, such as public TV stations? Would it be suitable for a world music station? A documentary station?

57. If you need more interviews, arrange them if possible.

58. Give the interviewee a copy of the finished product with the corrections. Make sure the interviewee signs a release form that he or she is satisfied with the corrections and is releasing the tape to you and your project.

59. Store the tapes and transcripts in a library or museum or at a university or other public place where it will be maintained and preserved for many generations and restored when necessary.

60. You can also send copies to a film repository or film library that takes video tapes, an archive for radio or audio tapes for radio broadcast or cable TV.

61. Copies may be sent to various archives for storage that lasts for many generations. Always ask whether there are facilities for restoring the tape. A museum would most likely have these provisions as would a large library that has an oral history library project or section.

62. Make sure the master copy is well protected and set up for long-term storage in a place where it will be protected and preserved.

63. If the oral history is about events in history, various network news TV stations might be interested. Film stock companies may be interested in copies of old photos.

64. Find out from the subject matter what type of archives, repository, or storage museums and libraries would be interested in receiving copies of the oral history tapes and transcripts.

65. Print media libraries would be interested in the hard paper copy transcripts and photos as would various ethnic associations and historical preservation societies. Find out whether the materials will go to microfiche, film, or be digitized and put on CDs and DVDs, or on the World Wide Web. If you want to create a time capsule for the Web, you can ask the interviewee whether he or she wants the materials or selected materials to be put online

or on CD as multimedia or other. Then you would get a signed release from the interviewee authorizing you to put the materials or excerpts online. Also find out in whose name the materials are copyrighted and whether you have print and electronic rights to the material or do the owners-authors-interviewees—or you, the videographer-producer? Get it all in writing, signed by those who have given you any interviews, even if you have to call your local intellectual property rights attorney.

Chapter Fourteen

How Accurate Are Plays and Monologues Based on Life Stories?

Have any stage play or oral history that is to be written as a skit or monologue recorded on video and audio. Autobiographies, biographies, personal histories, plays, and monologues present a *point of view.* Are all sides given equal emphasis? Will the audience choose favorite characters? Cameras give fragments, points of view, and bits and pieces. Viewers will see what the videographer or photographer intends to be seen. The interviewee will also be trying to put his point of view across and tell the story from his perspective.

Before you write for the stage with its lighting and sound effects in a very limited area, have someone videotape your rehearsal. Find out whether the videographer be in agreement with the interviewee? Or if you are recording for print transcript, will your point of view agree with the interviewee's perspective and experience if your basic 'premise,' where you two are coming from, are not in agreement? Think this over as you write your list of questions. Do both of you agree on your central issue on which you'll focus for the interview?

How are you going to turn spoken words into text for your paper hard copy transcript? Will you transcribe verbatim, correct the grammar, or quote as you hear the spoken words? Oral historians really need to transcribe the exact spoken word. You can leave out the 'ahs' and 'oms' or loud pauses, as the interviewee thinks what to say next. You don't want to sound like a court reporter, but you do want to have an accurate record transcribed of what was spoken.

When you write a play for the stage, the space and budget is very limited. So the sound and lighting effects must reflect a small auditorium or room. You can't have too much movement. A plane ride is simulated by one person in a chair. You can't have too many characters. About five or six characters is appropriate for a stage play, especially a play or skit with teenage characters.

If you're presenting a musical with dancing, you can have dancers or singers as in a choir or chorus, but for dramatic lines spoken, less is better. A monologue features one person speaking on a stage.

When writing a stage play, you're also not editing for a movie, unless you have permission to turn the oral history into a TV broadcast, where a lot gets cut out of the interview for time constraints. For that, you'd need written permission so words won't be taken out of context and strung together in the editing room to say something different from what the interviewee intended to say.

Someone talking could put in wrong names, forget what they wanted to say, or repeat themselves. They could mumble, ramble, or do almost anything. So you would have to sit down and weed out redundancy when you can or decide on presenting exactly what you've heard as transcript.

When someone reads the transcript in text, they won't have what you had in front of you, and they didn't see and hear the live presentation or the videotape. It's possible to misinterpret gestures or how something is spoken, the mood or tone, when reading a text transcript. Examine all your sources. Use an ice-breaker to get someone talking.

If a woman is talking about female-interest issues, she may feel more comfortable talking to another woman. Find out whether the interviewee is more comfortable speaking to someone of his or her own age. Some older persons feel they can relate better to someone close to their own age than someone in high school, but it varies. Sometimes older people can speak more freely to a teenager.

The interviewee must be able to feel comfortable with the interviewer and know he or she will not be judged. Sometimes it helps if the interviewer is the same ethnic group or there is someone present of the same group or if new to the language, a translator is present.

Read some books on oral history field techniques. Read the National Genealogical Society Quarterly (NGSQ). Also look at The American Genealogist (TAG), The Genealogist, and The New England Historical and Genealogical Register (The Register). If you don't know the maiden name of say, your grandmother's mother, and no relative knows either because it wasn't on her death certificate, try to reconstruct the lives of the males who had ever met the woman whose maiden name is unknown.

Maybe she did business with someone before marriage or went to school or court. Someone may have recorded the person's maiden name before her marriage. Try medical records if any were kept. There was no way to find my mother's grandmother's maiden name until I started searching to see whether she had any brothers in this country. She had to have come as a passenger on a ship around 1880 as she bought a farm. Did her husband come with her?

Was the farm in his name? How many brothers did she have in this country with her maiden surname? If the brothers were not in this country, what countries did they come from and what cities did they live in before they bought the farm in Albany? If I could find out what my great grandmother's maiden name was through any brothers living at the time, I could contact their descendants perhaps and see whether any male or female lines are still in this country or where else on the globe.

Perhaps a list of midwives in the village at the time is recorded in a church or training school for midwives. Fix the person in time and place. Find out whom she might have done business with and whether any records of that business exist. What businesses did she patronize? Look for divorce or court records, change of name records, and other legal documents.

Look at local sources. Did anyone save records from bills of sale for weddings, purchases of homes, furniture, debutante parties, infant supplies, or even medical records? Look at nurses' licenses, midwives' registers, employment contracts, and teachers' contracts, alumni associations for various schools, passports, passenger lists, alien registration cards, naturalization records, immigrant aid societies, city directories, and cross-references.

Try religious and women's clubs, lineage and village societies, girl scouts and similar groups, orphanages, sanatoriums, hospitals, police records. Years ago there was even a Eugenics Record Office. What about the women's prisons? The first one opened in 1839—Mount Pleasant Female Prison, NY.

Try voters' lists. If your relative is from another country, try records in those villages or cities abroad. Who kept the person's diaries? Have you checked the Orphan Train records? Try ethnic and religious societies and genealogy associations for that country. Most ethnic genealogy societies have a special interest group for even the smallest villages in various countries.

You can start one and put up a Web site for people who also come from there in past centuries. Check alimony, divorce, and court records, widow's pensions of veterans, adoptions, orphanages, foster homes, medical records, birth, marriage, and death certificates, social security, immigration, pet license owners' files, prisons, alumni groups from schools, passenger lists, military, and other legal records.

When all historical records are being tied together, you can add the DNA testing to link all those cousins. Check military pensions on microfilms in the National Archives. See the bibliography section of this book for further resources on highly recommended books and articles on oral history field techniques and similar historical subjects.

Chapter Fifteen

How to Use Evidence to Write Historical, Current Events, or Social Issues Slice of Life Plays, Skits, and Monologues

Writing Plays for High-School Students, Families, and Mature Adults from Life Stories and Personal Histories: Working with the Evidence

Plays, skits, and monologues based on slice-of-life vignettes or family stories are *evidence* of who we are. 'Salable' life stories usually are launched in the media—the major national press of credible repute—before they are produced as a video or movie and published as a book.

High-school and family skits, like corporate histories, may end up as time capsules on disk and on Web sites as video and audio documentaries or in books. Time capsules may contain personal histories, corporate histories, and even DNA-driven genealogy reports along with keepsake memorabilia. Material is documented on video, audio, and in text format. It's truly a multimedia production. Oral history tapes are transcribed and archived in libraries and museums. Here's how to document your personal history and launch a salable life story.

Write and produce as a video or audio your personal or oral history. Or present a folkloric tradition. Your salable life story can be presented as a time capsule, disk, Web site and keepsake album. The format may be a dramatic script, book, article, story, skit, radio broadcast, diary, novel, letter, article, monologue, or poem. Or cut and paste the text file into synthetic voice software and have it read and saved in your computer in most languages or with selected male or female voices or regional accents. Then 'burn' it to a DVD, CD, or any other format. Your life story is now saved in multimedia as a time capsule.

Before you think about publishing your life story or anyone else's, launch the personal history in the media. If you are working with someone else's life story, you'll need a signed release form allowing you to put the story on your Web site and/or on disk.

Be sure your form releases you from liability resulting from someone else's name going public for educational and scholarly research. Start with your own personal history and learn what pitfalls to avoid. Gain insight, foresight, and hindsight. Personal and oral history taping and archiving also branches into fields such as folklore and oral tradition, anthropology and ethnology. A personal historian can be an employee or an independent contractor. You can transcribe oral history tapes or work with creating audio and video files from your already written book or story.

Write Plays for Junior and Senior High-School Students or Senior Citizens

So you want to write a life story as a play or monologue? You are worth the storage. Launch your own personal history business by first doing a personal history on yourself and members of your family. You can include corporate histories, success story case histories, and life story writing circles for individuals. When somebody asks you for the facts, the primary source for research on your life story, only you can supply the evidence. This evidence is valuable. It's all about who you are, what you stand for, and how you reached out to others.

Showcase your own life history for your family, friends, or historians. Your life story is valuable now and in the distant future. You are part of history. Make sure a release form goes into your time capsule with your multimedia wishes concerning your life story in any format.

Maybe you'd also like to make time capsules? What about including DNA-driven genealogy reports as keepsake memorabilia? Include life stories, genealogy records, oral traditions, and folkloric customs. What's more valuable than a life story? You can focus on intergenerational writing, autobiographies, diaries, journals, video biographies, oral histories, corporate histories, tales, oral history tape transcribing. Or concentrate on life story writing in the form of books, video, audio, Web sites, skits, poems, memoirs, creative writing, greeting card CDs, DVD and video productions. Transfer tapes to disk. Design Web video broadcasting or make time capsules.

Write your own personal history. How do you write and launch salable life stories in the media, in the publishing world, and in the world of video, multi-media, Internet multicasting, Web-based historical documentaries, life-story-based novels, and film?

Every life story has four seasons and twelve stages like the months in a year. The four seasons are infancy, childhood, adulthood, and grace-age. Or you want to be an oral traditionalist, folklorist, or oral historian, folklore librarian, or archivist and conservator of old videos, photos, letters, articles, disks, and books. What makes your personal history salable? Marketability is born in the national media. Credible journalism launches your story to agents, entertainment attorneys, publishers and producers long before your book is published or your video is made available to the public through your Web site, DVD, CD greeting card, or other time capsule.

Maybe you want to know how to promote and publicize life stories in the media before they are published as books or produced cinematically. Or you want to write, promote, and sell your autobiography—commercially—to a selected niche market audience.

Personal histories are found in books, video, film, audio, and games. Depending upon your field of focus, your autobiography or anyone else's life story can become a salable personal history. A life story becomes 'commercial' or salable when it is launched in the national press before it is published as a book or produced as a movie or video.

It also can become a time capsule on disk and/or on an Internet Web site. An audio or video tape on the Web is part of a personal broadcasting network. Personal and corporate histories are time capsules. Oral histories may be transcribed into text.

Text writings may be imported or cut and pasted into synthetic voice software and quickly turned into audio files, DVDs, CDs, or tapes and uploaded to a Web site to be broadcast much like a personal radio station or broadcasting network. Audio or video files can be uploaded to Web sites and download to personal computers anywhere in the world with Internet access. The files can be saved by right-clicking a computer mouse and "saved as a target" in anyone's computer and then played on a computer hard disk drive or saved to other disks or transferred to tapes or DVDs or CDs or most any other media.

Live voices or synthetic software voices can read text and be saved as a computer file much the same as any audio or video file. And to make sure text stays as readable text, books of all sizes or skits and plays or scripts can be written or transcribed from oral interviews of anyone's life story. The same may be done for the oral history of a corporation, or for folklore tradition. It's all part of a career as a personal and/or oral historian. Here, anthropology, history, ethnology, creative writing, genealogy, and public speaking combine. You can even put printouts and reports of DNA-driven genealogy research on a person or family in a genealogy-related time capsule to be opened by future generations.

In the time capsule could be video and audio material, text writings, diaries, oral traditions, and anything related to life story writing. Keepsakes and poetry, dramatizations, skits, plays, and the reminiscing of individuals, groups, or corporations may go into a time capsule. What used to be keepsake albums (scrap-books) can now become time capsules.

If you want to be a personal historian, you can open an independent business where you travel in an area in order to 'videotape' people with your camcorder, usually in digital high 8 format, and transcribe the tapes to appear as text transcripts of what they said orally on the video or audio tape, CD, or DVD.

You can spend up to six hours transcribing a one-hour video or audio tape. Often there are two voices, the interviewer and the interviewee on the tape. Some people may want to speak into a tape recorder or camcorder and tape themselves when they are alone in a room without an interviewer. These people would receive a list of questions to look at so they can answer focusing on turning points or highlight the significant events in their lives.

You may want to tape a group of people speaking for five to seven minutes each on a special topic such as what did you do during World War II? Maybe the people in the group would describe what it was like living in a certain place during a certain decade or working in a certain environment or occupation.

Life story tapes usually run about an hour for individuals to talk about their entire life history in five minute segments. Fifteen five-minute segments can bring them up to age seventy-five. These can be taped weekly or daily during a fifteen-week 'semester' or fifteen days of daily taping where they speak in five-minute 'chunks' on one videotape.

The five minute segments allows art work, photos, slides, or video clips of other scenes, such as the house they live in or anything pertinent to be taped or photographed and edited in between segments. A personal history taping can run as a 15-week class in life story writing. For those who don't want to appear on camera, audio tape can be used in a tape recorder.

Most people find it difficult to sit in front of a camcorder for one hour and continuously speak or answer questions. Some enjoy an interview that does last an hour. Others would rather use the five-minute segments and have you tape them in a classroom setting or their home another day, perhaps each day at the same time during a 15-week 'semester.'

Personal history may be done as an adult education course in any type of setting from recreation room of an assisted living facility or senior community center to a private home or public classroom in an adult education class in life story writing. If you're running a class, you might have the people meet from 11 am to noon each Sunday, perhaps right after their 10 am church service for a taping.

Each person can spend as much time as he or she wants—either one five-minute segment or perhaps three segments totaling fifteen minutes each week until the one-hour tape is completed. You can include, if desired, a DNA-driven genealogy report in case the person wants a DNA test for ancestry to put into a time capsule for family members and future generations.

The time capsule would contain a text version of the life story of each member of the family or of one individual. It would also have a video tape, an audio tape, any keepsakes, and the creative work such as poetry or skits and writings or art work, photos, and other memorabilia that can fit into the time capsule.

A video or audio tape would also be preserved on a DVD and a CD, and if possible, uploaded to a Web site as a video and/or audio file of the individual or one of the family members who has access to the Internet and can purchase Web site space allowing a video and audio file to be uploaded along with the text transcription or life story writing of the individual. This makes a wonderful time capsule gift in personal history.

You'll want to know how to write it so that it can be marketed to your niche customers or audience. Maybe you'll combine your personal history with a practical invention of some type, such as an inexpensive device everyone can use or a special cooking utensil. This book is about becoming a personal historian. From there, your works can diverge into many roads or branches that link back to personal history.

Why do you want to write a personal history of someone or an autobiography of yourself and make it commercial to sell to a niche or wide audience? You may want to flummox the readers and enhance their public or private lives.

You may want to protect an institution from mockery. Or you want to take a stand and speak in codes that are the shorthand of living. To be concrete, writing and/or producing or transcribing personal history, oral history, folklore and oral tradition may focus on taking a stand on specific areas of life such as recording your experience being bullied in elementary school and focusing on taking a stand by writing a series of teaching guides with a training videotape or disk featuring your personal history and the personal histories of others with similar past experiences.

Maybe you want to join your personal history with others' personal histories in a documentary disk or tape defending a symbol of religious or ethnic identity. Should you wear that symbol in public, for example, in school or at work or during travel? Should you defend that symbol with a time capsule, an oral history, or personal history videotape, DVD, and text material? On your Web site in multimedia? In a keepsake album?

In what do you seek comfort? Your personal history can be about seeking comfort in food, work, play, care giving, leisure, travel, research, art, writing, or whatever you choose. What's your crusade about and how would you describe or show your slogan?

If you write a commercial autobiography, you'll want to know how to market your work. You might wish to make time capsules to preserve the highlights of life stories of older adults or corporations. You can carve out a career as a personal historian and interview people, record what they say on a variety of media, and have the tapes transcribed to text or transcribe them yourself.

You can conserve paper or videos, transfer the medium to new technologies such as video tape to DVD disks, or make keepsake albums and multimedia time capsules. 'Scrap booking' can become oral tradition or personal history as a play or skit.

What you're creating are keepsakes or time capsules. And what is a keepsake to the average person becomes a time capsule to an oral historian and archaeologist. You can even include DNA-driven genealogy reports in a keepsake or time capsule.

Maybe you want to write commercial biographies or your autobiography. Perhaps you'll ghostwrite other people's autobiographies. Or you'll perhaps choose to write corporate biographies and success stories and be a case history manager or consultant for new companies. You can transcribe oral histories. Another route is to produce or tape video biographies and archive them in oral history libraries, usually at universities, museums, or other foundation.

Chapter Sixteen

What Makes a Life Story Excerpt or Highlight Salable as a One-Act Play or Skit?

Q. What makes a life story saleable as a high-school play, skit, or monologue?
A. The buzz appeal of a high velocity personal memoir with teenage characters is most appealing to high-school drama teachers. A life story as a play is salable when it has universal appeal and identity. An example is a single parent making great sacrifices to put bread on the table and raise a decent family in hard times. Many people identify with the universal theme of a life story. Buzz appeal draws in the deep interest of the press to publicize and lend credibility to a life story, to put a spin on it in the media, and to sell it to the public because all readers may be able to see themselves in your life story.

Q. To whom do you sell your life story to?
A. You sell your life story to publishers specializing in life stories. If you look under biographies in a book such as Writer's Guide to Book Editors, Publishers, and Literary Agents, 1999-2000, by Jeff Herman, Prima Publishing, you'll see several pages of publishers of life story, biography, and memoirs or autobiography.
A few include The Anonymous Press, Andrews McMeel Publishing, Applause Theatre Book Publishers, Barricade Books, Inc., Baskerville Publishers, and many more listed in that directory. Also take a look at Writers Market, Writers Digest Books, checkout Memoirs in the index. Publishers include Feminist Press, Hachai, Hollis, Narwhal, Northeastern University Press, Puppy House,

Westminster, John Knox,and others. Check categories such as creative nonfiction, biography, ethnic, historical, multicultural and other categories for lists of publishers in your genre. Don't overlook writing your life story as a play, monologue, or script or for the audio book market.

Q. How do you present your life story in order to turn it into a saleable book, article, play, or other type of literature so that other people will want to read it?
A. You write a high-velocity powerful personal memoir or autonomedia which emphasizes cultural criticism and theory. Or you write a factual expose, keep a journal on the current cultural pulse, or write a diary about what it feels like to be single and dating in your age group—thirty something, sixty-something, or whatever you choose. You become an investigative biographer. You write a riveting love story. Or how to use love to heal. Or you write about breaking through old barriers to create new publishing frontiers.

Q. How do you write a commercial biography?
A. Make sure someone wants to buy it before you write the whole thing. The details will be forthcoming in the course as it begins. Then contact the press, reporters in the media with credibility who write for a national daily newspaper or reputable magazine. Also contact radio and cable TV stations to do interviews on a selected event in your life story or biography. Pick a niche market where the particular audience has a special interest in that experience.

Q. The difference between authorized and unauthorized.
A. Authorized means you have permission and approval from the person about whom you're writing.

Q. Who gets assigned to write biographies of celebrities or other famous people?
A. Usually newspaper columnists who cover the beat or subject area, or you're a known writer who contacts an agent specializing in writing or ghostwriting celebrity biographies. You can enter this profession from many doors. I'll explain in the course.

Writing Your Ending First Gives You Closure And Clues How To Solve The Problems In Your Life Story. Teaching Life Story Writing On The Internet

When you write a salable life story, it's easier to write your ending first. Eventually, with experience working with a variety of life stories, you can start quality circles or classes in life story writing (writing your salable memoirs, autobiography, biography, corporate history, family history, your diary as a commercial novel or play or true confession, true story, or true crime book or story or script).

Also, you can teach playwriting as life story writing, interviewing, or videobiography on the Internet for yourself or for an existing school or program. It's relaxing and comforting to sit at home in perfect quiet and type a lecture into a screen browser such as the courses that can be offered through www.blackboard.com and other programs. Or teach online using a live chat screen.

Customize your course to the needs of your students. You may need certification or a graduate degree to teach for a university online, but there's also adult education classes given in nontraditional settings such as churches, libraries, and museums.

Online, you can offer independent classes and go into business for yourself as a personal historian. Another way is to offer time capsules, keepsake albums, gift baskets, greeting cards, life stories on video, DVD, or transcribed from oral history. Work with libraries, museums, or your own independent classes.

You can work at home or be mobile and travel to other people's homes or senior centers and assisted living recreation rooms, community centers, or schools and theaters to work with life stories. Some companies have put life-story recording kiosks in public places such as train stations or airports.

Check out the StoryCorps Web site at http://www.storycorps.net/. Find your own mission or purpose and create your own business recording the life stories of a variety of people in video, sound, text, or multimedia formats. It's all part of the time-capsule generation that emphasizes your life story has value and needs to be preserved as part of history.

The revelation is that your life story isn't only for your family and friends anymore. As part of history, the world can now experience the one universal that connects us—life, and within a life story—insight, foresight, and hindsight.

Diaries of senior citizens are in demand. To sell them, you need buzz appeal, visibility in the press for writing simple stories of how you struggled to put bread on the table and raised a family alone, or what you've learned from your mistakes or experiences, how you solved problems, gave yourself more choices, grew, and came to understand why you were transformed. People are looking for universal experiences to help them make decisions.

Start by finding a newspaper reporter from a publication that is well-respected by the public, and have that person write about your life story experience or what you do with other peoples' life stories as a personal historian. That's the first step to introducing a 'salable' life story.

The technique differs from writing a life story like a first-person diary novel for only your family and/or friends. With a 'salable' life story, you write about the universal experiences that connect all of us. If readers or viewers can identify with what you have to say, your words open doors for them to make decisions and choices by digesting your information.

The Proliferation of Playwriting Courses Online Targets Writing Your Life Story

The sheer number of classes on the Internet is like an explosion of education. You can now earn a masters degree in the techniques of teaching online from universities such as the California State University at Hayward in their continuing education department. What I see happening is that according to display ads in a variety of magazines of interest to writers, a proliferation of writing courses online has broken out.

How do you develop buzz appeal, pre-sell your book, create press coverage of their writing, all before you send it to a publisher or agent? A few years ago diaries were "in" just like several years before that the books about angels were "in style." What will be next?

Back in the year 2000, what enthralled readers included simple stories on how single parents put bread on the table, reared a family, and learned from their mistakes. What will be big in the future in publishing will be simple tales of what you learned, how you came to understand, and what you'll share with readers because what you learned from my mistakes helped you to grow and become a better person making the world a gentler place. Those books will be about values, virtues, and ethics in simple stories that help people heal. It will be universal stories with which we all can identify and use to solve problems and make decisions.

By the following year books showed readers how to have more choices and find more alternative solutions, more possibilities, and to find more information with which to solve problems and make decisions. A lot of those books will come from salable diaries and life stories as well as corporate histories and executive histories.

What was hot by 2002 was how people escaped domestic violence and made better choices through education and creativity enhancement. By 2003-2004 books focused on creativity enhancement and self-expression. The year 2003 became a utopia for books on creativity enhancement through personal experience and life story. You only have to look at the book lists in the publisher's magazines to see what the fad is for any one year and interview publishing professionals for the trends and directions for the following year.

Write about the human side of careers worked at for years. What did you retire to? How did you survive historic events, rear your family, or solve problems?

The purpose of personal history writing can be, among other goals, to find closure. Those who can't use a hand-operated mouse and need to use a foot pedal mouse, breath straw, or other devices can still operate computers. Others need assistance software to magnify the screen or audio software such as "Jaws," to hear as they type on keyboards.

The idea is to use personal history and life story writing as a healing instrument to make contact with others, find this closure, relieve stress, to talk to parents long gone, to make decisions on how to grow, find understanding, learn from past mistakes, grow, and become a better person in one's own eyes.

Other students take a personal history, oral history, or life story writing classes to pass on to their grandchildren a script, a novel, a story, or a collage of their life experiences, and still others want corporate histories of how they founded their companies and became role models of success for business students to simulate, how they became successful giants for others to follow and benchmark.

Still other students are visionaries who want their life stories to be used to enhance the creativity of readers. Some of my students want to write their life story as a computer or board game on how they solved their own problems that are universal to all of us. And you have students who want careers as personal historians recording, transcribing, and preserving in a variety of formats the personal histories of individuals, families, corporations, art forms, and institutions.

Some are into conservation of videos, photographs, text material, tape recordings, CDs, DVDs, and other multimedia formats. All are involved in making time capsules for future researchers, historians, scholars, librarians, genealogists, and specialists who research personal and oral history or specialized history, such as music and art or rare books and manuscripts. Others are collectors. Most want a time capsule of a relative, complete with not only a relative's keepsake albums or video diary, but sometimes even a DNA printout for ancestry.

If you look in many publications of interest to writers, you might see online or correspondence courses offered to writers at American College of Journalism, Burlington College, Columbus University, specialists in distance education, or at Gotham Writers' Workshops at www.WritingClasses.com. There's Writers Digest School, and data bases where you can learn about agents at Agent Research & Evaluation, 334 E. 30, NYC, NY 10016 or on the Web at www.agentresearch.com. These are some of the online classes in writing advertised. You'll also see ads for classes in personal story writing in some of these publications.

You can get paid to teach what you love to do so much—share your writing techniques and write. Some writing schools online may put articles up on their trade journal online. And you can always sell articles to paying markets and use the clips with resumes. Thanks to the Internet—even a disabled teacher who isn't able to speak before a class for health reasons or drive to class, can teach and write online.

Personal history writing courses could also aim to show research on how creative writing can heal or have therapeutic qualities in gentle self-expression and quality circles online, and now I've found students who learn how to write a life story as therapy to heal and to find closure, solve problems, and to explore more choices, alternatives, and growth towards a kinder and gentler world.

You can focus strictly on recording, transcribing, and archiving people's or corporation's personal or oral histories and preserving them in a variety of formats as time capsules or target the more creative end of teaching writing personal histories as books, plays, or skits. In other words, you can be both a personal historian and a writing coach or focus on either career or business—oral and personal historian, or teacher of courses or "quality circles" in writing autobiographies and biographies for commercial markets.

You can start private classes on a mailing list and chat board. A fair price to charge could be about $80 per student for advanced workshops in writing salable material for 4-week courses with a 10-page critique per student. Your aim would be to be an online job coach in a writing or personal history career. Help students find ways to get into print by referring you them to resources. Show how to make writing more commercial. Reveal the techniques of effective story writing in your true story, biography, memoirs, autobiography, diary, journal, novel, story, play, or article.

A lot of biography writing is focused on interviews, whereas writing a diary or monologue focuses on inner reflections and expressions in explaining how you came to understand, learn from your past mistakes or experiences and good choices, and share how you solved problems, grew, and changed or were transformed.

Personal diaries start out with poetic-like descriptions of the senses, with lines such as "Cat shadow plump I arrive, carrying my Siamese kitten like a rifle through Spokane, while the only sensation I feel is my hair stretched like flaxen wires where my new kitten, Patches, hangs on. A gentle clock, the red beams of light reflected in his blue eyes remind me that my tattered self also must eat. His claws dig into my purse strap like golden flowers curling in unshaven armpits. I inhale his purrs like garlic, warm as the pap mom cat, Rada-Ring flowed into Patches nine weeks ago."

Have an enriching writing experience. I truly believe writing heals in some ways. It's a transformative experience like meditation or having the comforting feeling of watching a waterfall in natural settings or sitting in a garden of hanging green plants. Writing recharges my energy must like petting my kitten, Kokowellen, a Siamese while sitting my orchid garden listening to soothing melodies.

You might want to critique for pay, the pages of other people's writing of personal histories if they want to write for the commercial markets. In that case, critiquing may be done by email and online. That way they don't send any hard copy to mail back or get lost. You always keep a copy. However, I recommend teaching online a course with the critique, as you'll get far more for your $80 for each ten pages of critiquing as a fair price, plus the tuition of the course as perhaps another $80.

The course provides resources, techniques, and ways to revise your material that helps you gain visibility. It's important to pre-sell your book and gain publicity for your writing before you send it off to a publisher or agent. You'll want to know how not to give too much away, but how to attract positive attention so people will eagerly look forward to hearing more from you.

Keep a separate mailing list for your online students. Make a mailing list. Plays or monologues written from memoirs and diaries or excerpts and highlights of life stories are in right now in the publishing world. It's not a passed fad, yet, like the angel books were a decade ago. If you're writing a diary, you want to write something in your first or second page after the opening that goes like this to be more commercial:

"Eagerness to learn grows on me. I see it reflected in the interviewers who stare at me. Their enthusiasm is an approval of my expansive mind. I read so much now, just to look at the pages is to feel nourished. A kind of poetry turns into children's books on DVDs like a stalk that grows no where else is in season.

Creativity, like color, runs off my keyboard into the cooking water of my screen, drenched in pungent brainstorming. Writing online puts me in every farmer's kitchen. My computer has a good scent, and the stories written on its screen are apples bursting on the trees of my fingers. On my Web site, photos hang like lanterns. Teaching online ripens my stories. I analyze what effective storytelling means. Picture pagodas of the mind in three dimensions."

If you come across writers block, try writing the lyrics to a song as a way to start writing your life story. You don't need to read notes, just fiddle with the words based upon an experience in time. Start by writing the ending first. Perhaps your title on salable diaries could be, "Pretty Little Secret," or "Ending the Silence," or "Results of Promises," or "Guided by a Child's Silence," or "Unraveling a Tale," or "Bravery and Unspeakable Links," or "Unveiled, Unbridled, Unbound." My title was "Insight, Hindsight, Foresight."

Chapter Seventeen

Turning Plays and Skits into Computer and Board Games

The goal of fiction writers in the new media is to adapt your story, novel, or script to as many platforms, formats and media as possible and to sell to multiple markets—either online, multi-casting, or multimedia. Computer game scripts aren't only for computer games anymore.

They're used in dramatizations for training and learning simulations and other learning materials as well as for entertainment online, on disk, and for infotainment and edutainment at all levels from corporate training to Web sites for children and young adults, seniors, and students.

Here's how to write a computer game script that you can adapt to any type of simulation training or interactive learning as well as entertainment fiction. The average computer screen interactive video or game has double the number of camera directions as a regular video script. The increased number of descriptions account for the camera directions and the director's directions (since you're the director and the writer on the computer as you are in animation).

So to adapt your screenplay to the new media, separate the beginning, middle and ending exactly as you would cut off the beginning, middle, and ending of a short story or novel. In a screenplay, every scene forms a creative concept. In the industry, the executives try to separate the one-line high concept from the whole-story-based creative concept.

A creative concept is a basic device that's used like an all-encompassing net to catch all the important events of the story. Think of your creative concept as a native American dream catcher net full of feathers and beads woven into memories and facts of your story. Its one purpose is to grab the audience's attention and squeeze until it gives pleasure or emotional response, like fear.

Summarize the highlights into a single paragraph that tells the story. In a screenplay, it has been said and for the past two decades been written about that you divide your story into three acts. However, in adapting a script or story to the new interactive media, you don't divide it into three acts, and you don't divide it into six acts. You bring out eight octopus-sized tentacles or branches and you hang your computer game script or interactive book story on those eight branches.

It has been said that at each new path, or what the screenplay books of the seventies used to call turning points, a new crisis happens that propels the action in forward. However, in the new media, each new crisis instead propels the action down another branching pathway, through another road, and into another narrative.

Again, the reader chooses when the action is supposed to branch and turn on its dime to move forward in not so much a new direction, but in the direction the reader says it will move. The writer no longer chooses. Interactively, the reader chooses.

If you need to write a premise and introduce your hero, in an interactive script you adapt your old media book by writing a summary of the end first and then working backwards to the first chapter or the first page. Interactive books are adapted by writing back starting with the end of the book, story, or script and shuffling the deck.

The crisis that sets the story in motion is never limited to only one crisis, but eight, or four, or two, or some other even number. Let the reader choose the crisis the viewer wants to work with, and give more than one summary of each chapter. You adapt a life story to a play, skit, monologue, or script to the new media by working backwards from the end of the adventure.

Here are some problems to solve as you write your dramatizations or plays and skits for training scripts online or computer game scripts:

- In a nonfiction interactive script, find your biggest weapon to slay the problem that has to be solved in the action of your nonfiction script. This cliffhanger approach is good when you're writing a how-to training video, film, or CD-ROM learning tool.
- Create a high-stakes races to hook your cliffhanger on.
- Find a new acronym for each 7-minute scene in your script and lay your cliffhanger on at the end of each 7-8 minute segment of a nonfiction script.

- If you're looking for a cover-all that makes your script hang together, use the cliffhanger to make a connection between what's a household name in your script, the problem to be solved, and the method your narrator or main character uses in the dramatization to solve the problem and reach a conclusion.
- Sell your cliffhangers to the interactive TV market targeting ADSL (asymmetric digital subscriber line) technology. ADSL is high bandwidth Internet connectivity that you can use to bring your script to commercial quality video on the Web. Use videoconferencing as a means to transmit your scripts to a live audience interested in nonfiction—that is problem solving, skill training, test taking/preparation, and feedback at business meetings.
- Use wireless paths to sell your cliffhangers, and use cliffhangers in training videos and videoconferencing. The phone companies are eager to get into the interactive TV business.
- Write scripts about bandwidth itself for a technical audience as practice, using cliffhangers every 7-8 minutes as paths provided for the narrator to take new action and move the script faster until a problem is solved at the end and the skill is learned by the corporate employee or student watching your script.
- Have your script read before a live audience or through videoconferencing and have the audience decide which cliffhangers to insert at each point. Use about 8 cliffhangers per instructional film script.
- Cliffhangers can be used in nonfiction comic books or graphic instructional materials. Most comic books are 32 pages in length. Double that size to 64 pages and you come out with a script for a computer game lasting 22 minutes or more. You also get a graphic novel at that length or a booklet on how to perform a special skill.

The competing cliffhangers grow in volume as the story moves forward, even if it's a routine safety instructional film to train vehicle drivers. Test your cliffhangers' performance. Set up a Web site and get feedback from your cliffhangers from an audience. Try before you make your cliffhangers permanent.

You're teaching even if you're not writing anything instructional in the traditional sense. Propaganda films teach a lesson, too. You get at the emotional response of the audience through cliffhangers. Then you appeal to their thinking, logical side to insert the facts that come after the cliffhanger. The narrator, the product, or the audience can become involved n the cliffhanger and solve the problem to get the answer. Use mazes when appropriate.

Even mazes can become cliffhangers, and text mazes of logic are useful only when you are teaching the viewer to use test methods to solve problems. Write cliffhangers as plays. Use more emotion than you would in a film script.

Don't insist the audience will think if they are looking to escape and feel. You're not writing a film script with outdoor action. Most people view a script to have fun and learn by passive imprinting and associations rather than to be forced to solve problems.

Therefore, let the dramatized character solve the cliffhanger/problem. A cliffhanger is a substitute for a problem to be solved in a nonfiction script. In a fiction script, a cliffhanger is hidden problem to be solved and exposed suspense requiring emotional reactions to solve.

Ten Steps to Dramatizing Interactive Personal Essays as Plays

1. Ask a specific question.
2. Use the essay to answer the question.
3. Write the question at the start of the essay and make your question interactive inserting many branches or possibilities each possibility narrowing down more and more to concentrate your reader's mind.
4. Use the interactivity to ask the reader how does this paragraph help answer the question?
5. Whenever the paragraph finishes answering the question begin a new branching narrative, pathway, or choice for the reader. It's time for a break of concentration and a shifting to a cliff-hanger.
6. Even the brief personal essays in interactive media can have cliffhangers, even in nonfiction, autobiography, and other personal essays based on life experience. Many experiences can lead to a topic for writing in any media, such as how to receive email interviews.
7. Another fiction with a real-life practical use online topic you can make a script or article from is how to get terrific email interviews. Books can be written from lists such as a list fleshed out of what are the funniest things that happened to employers recruiting employees on the Internet, such as viruses that came with resumes. Base your writing on interviews with dozens of human resources personnel who hire people from the Internet based on resumes and correspondence coming in my email and from Web page recruiting.

8. A writer gets all interviews for a book from the Internet. I once wrote a book based on interviews all gotten by email. I requested the interview by email and got the person on the other side to give me the interview by email only.

9. Most of my interviews in the past were with famous and best selling authors and screenwriters, including interviews with big-name screenwriters who switched to writing for the new media (like Ken Goldstein, publisher/screenwriter of the Carmen San Diego series for Broderbund), and best selling interactive novel writers/publishers, and virtual press publishers.

10. You could write a computer game, animation script, essay or an article or book on how to get great interviews by email for any writer who is working on a book or a column. Your title could be: Secrets of Success in Email Interviewing. What\'s the funniest thing that happened to you on the Internet while writing your column or other creative writing?

Interview
Jeffrey Sullivan of DigitalArcana, Inc.
http://www.DigitalArcana.com

What outlook do you see in interactive multimedia for freelance fiction and/or nonfiction writers as far as making a living, opening a writing service or home-based business, or getting a job?

There is tremendous opportunity for writers (both fiction and non-fiction) in the area of interactive media. The incredible growth in the market has spawned a strong appetite for new talent, and the increasing market shares in the more mature sub-markets mean some increase in pay rates. Building a career in this field remains a fantastic opportunity, but there are some things to remember:

1. Know your field. Don't just hop on the bandwagon because you hear interactive is "the next hot thing." Not only will it be easy for potential employers to sniff this out, but it's the absolute worst thing you can do, both for your personal employment opportunities, and for opportunities for writers in general.

2. One of the biggest problems in interactive is that there are a lot of "displaced writers" from other media who figure that "writing is writing," so they just hop into interactive, over-promise what they can do in this tricky medium, and leave producers with a bad taste in their mouth for "professional writers."

3. The newer the field, the more appetite, but the less the pay (in general). If you want to be on the cutting edge, be prepared to pay the dues.

4.   Love this stuff. If you're just in it for a paycheck, then #1-2 above will ensure that you not only flop, but that you make it harder for other writers to follow you.

Solid writing skills is something I'll take as a given (if you don't have it, I can't tell you how to get it). Experience is easy to acquire. Go out there and use the products you want to create. If it's adventure games, play adventure games ravenously. If it's edutainment, then experience all of them out there.

One caveat: don't just check out the "hot" titles in a field. There's nothing worse than hearing a person rattle off the two or three best known entries in a field as their favorites, a sure sign that they haven't done their homework. (A side note: if I had a dime for every time I heard someone tell me they had an idea for a cross between "Doom" and "MYST" over the past few years, I'd be independently wealthy.)

For the older writer—55+—who has been rejected by ageism from the Hollywood screenwriting market, or for the novelist seeking a publisher, what does interactive multimedia offer?

I hate to say this, but in many of the interactive fields, ageism is even worse in interactive. In all of the "hot" areas like cutting-edge gaming and interactive fiction, there is a fairly strong perception that anyone over the age of 30 (!) doesn't "get it," and can't write this stuff.

The perception is that well-established linear writers simply can't think non-linearly as interactive often requires. However, I think that in the fields of reference, education, and entertainment, there may be much less of this attitude. Since my experience lies elsewhere, however, I can't be sure.

How would a freelance writer of fiction or nonfiction who has been doing print writing for years begin to make the leap to get into writing interactive multimedia? Are there any jobs out there for writers who can't find work on daily newspapers because of the downsizing of daily newspapers?

If you're a newspaper writer, your best entree into interactive may be with the marketing department of an interactive company; there your skills are the most directly relevant. Once you're in, you can absorb the culture and experience, and try to branch out into other areas.

For general writers, the key is knowing the field. Know as much as you can about what has worked (and what has not) in your field, and know why things work or don't, in your opinion. Knowledgeable people in this field are rare, so preparing yourself is a great way to get that foot a little farther in the door.

What advice would you give to creative writers of all types to enter the new media?

Know the area you want to work in exhaustively. And try to know the other areas at least in passing. You never know where a good idea (or even a bad one) in one field will yield a great innovation in another.
Is there anything readers might want to know about the hidden markets in interactive multimedia? Can one work at home?
Working at home is a definite option in many cases. Interactive firms, being much more highly computerized in general, are a lot more comfortable with the concept of telecommuting or simply working off-site than many other industries.

Is it easier to sell to the interactive multimedia market than to try to find a print publisher for one's novel, screenplay, or how-to nonfiction book?

No. With respect to a book, you can create what is essentially the finished product. with respect to a screenplay, even though the script isn't the finished product, the accepted convention is that writers don't do anything more than a script. In interactive, however, the norm is to need to do a prototype or sample art in addition to a design document, so there is more to do to get an idea sold. Add to that the fact that many companies have more ideas than they can handle, and the market for new ideas is not as great as it once was.

What education is best for a freelance creative writer to get a foot in the door in the new media? A background in computers, writing, game playing (if you're interested in the game market).

Can a writer educate himself at home and work at home, or must there be a college degree with a major in interactive multimedia to enter the occupation of writer in this field? In other words, will a B.A. in English get one in the door? What other job titles are there in interactive multimedia for writers? What else can they do in this field to find work? How long have writers been writing for interactive multimedia? Five years? Three years?

Absolutely not. For one thing, these college degrees are so new that there are few people in the market who will even have one. Second, this industry values credits and experience over degrees more than many other fields. The more technical your interest, however, the more likely that a degree will be necessary.

What's the future of multimedia for freelance creative writers?

I think that creative people will be the guiding force in moving interactive media into a new and mature mass-medium. Technology can only take you so far, and although we've been driven by it so far, it is becoming harder and harder to differentiate your product on technology alone. Soon, it will be impossible. The companies know this, but they are often caught between two cultures (technology driving product and content driving product); soon their minds will be made up for them.

*   *   *

Writing Multimedia Plays for High-School Students and Older Adults

*   *   *

What kind of training would a writer need to write real life story plays for multimedia or Internet Broadcasting?

The three key ingredients are solid experience in the following genres:

1.   Writing or adapting plays, skits, and monologues from real life stories.
2.   Working with interactive literature and multimedia skills.
3.   Oral and personal history interviewing skills.

*   *   *

Chapter Eighteen

Stimulating Memories for Plays, Skits, and Monologues

Does Writing Your Life Story As A Play for High-School Students or Older Adults Help Refresh Memories?

Keys: 1. Plug in characters to a variety of experiences.
           2. Research several ways to tell the same story.

Monologues, plays, and oral histories depend upon memory and the ability to speak. I also think of oral history as aural history, based on the ability to hear someone's experiences and remember them to pass on to the next generation or the world.

To find out the effects of oral history on memory and on creative writing of plays, skits, or stories on memory, we'd have to ask the people who write their life story and/or genealogy in their older years what it did for them, their memory, and their ability to think and feel. Make use of introverted feeling in writing a commercial or salable life story for the new media. Think in three dimensions for older adults is a different highway. How did DNA testing influence a genealogy search for family history facts?

Did the individual create a time capsule? How was the time capsule saved—on the Web? On a CD, DVD, video, or audio tape? In a scrapbook of photos, with various memorabilia? Did anyone rescue old photos from antique stores and flea markets by searching for photographer's prints on the front or back of the photo or names on the back of the photo and dates or locations?

1. When turning your salable life story, corporate history, or biography into an adventure action romance novel, don't set up your main characters in the first chapter to be in transit traveling on board a plane, train, or ship going somewhere. The action actually starts or hits them after they have already arrived at their destination.

Start your first chapter when your characters already get to their destination place or point in time. A first chapter that opens when your main character is on a plane or train is the kiss of death from many editors point of view and the main reason why a good novel often is rejected.

Cut out the traveling scene from your first chapter and begin where the action starts for real, at the destination point. Does anyone visit antique stores, malls, or flea markets to search for family history memorabilia? What about attic, basement, or garage sales?

2. Use a lot of dialogue when turning a biography or your life story into a salable novel, especially in a romance, adventure action, or suspense novel or in one where you combine romance with adventure and suspense.

Use no more than three pages of narrative without dialogue. Let characters speak through the dialogue and tell the reader what is happening. Get characters to speak as normally as possible. If the times and place dictate they speak in proverbs, so be it. Proverbs make the best novels as you turn your proverb into a story and play it out as a novel. Otherwise, have normal speech so you can be the catalyst and bring people together who understand clearly what one another means.

3. Put your characters on the stage and have them talking to one another. If you have introspection in your book, don't use introspection for your action line. Action adventure books keep characters on stage talking to the audience.

4. Use magazines and clothing catalogues to make a collage of what your character might look like. This inspiration may go up on a board in front of you or on the wall to see as you work. Get a picture in your mind of what your characters look like. If they don't exist in art history, draw them yourself or make a mixed media collage of what they look like, speak like, and stand for. Some ideas include the models in "cigar" magazines, catalogues, and fashion publications as well as multi-ethnic and historical illustrations and photos.

5. Research history and keep a loose-leaf notebook with tabs on the history of places you want to research. The history itself is great for ideas on what plot to write. Look at or visit old forts and similar places. Plug in characters to your research. Look at forts of foreign settlements in the country of your choice, U.S. or any other place. Record the dates in your files. Create a spreadsheet in Excel or any other type of spread sheet with your dates from historical research as these will relate to your characters and help you develop a real plot.

6. Keep a notebook for each novel or biography you write. Put everything related to each book in a notebook. Have one notebook for historical research and one for the novel you're writing or true storybook.

7. When sending out your book manuscript make a media kit for yourself with your resume, photo, list of works in development if you are not yet published, and any other material about your own experience in any other field. Your own biography and photo presented to the press also can be used to let an editor know when you send out your manuscript of what's in development and what you've done.

8. Write down the point of view before your book is begun. Whose point of view is it anyway? Who tells the story? If you're writing a romance novel from your life story or a military romantic suspense novel, true story, radio script, or other genre, agree on the point of view before you start.

9. Who will tell the story, and how does the individual know how the other characters know what to say?

10. It is not necessary to continue ethnic stereotypes in your book. If one of your characters is a music agent, for example, and a lot of music agents are of one ethnicity or speak with a certain accent, it's not necessary to continue the stereotyping roles. Pick something new for a change.

11. Cliché use evokes familiarity, especially in a title. Research many different ways to tell the same story. Use plays, skits, monologues, dramatizations, diaries, novels, stories, and essays. Viewers and readers need to grasp facts or experiences, anecdotes, oral histories, and stories that have not been generalized. Use a series of incidents, action and relationship tension to balance your plot with your dialogue. Transcribe recorded oral histories. Use a release form that releases you from liability resulting from any public viewing.

12. If you're turning a biography into a romance novel, you need to balance the relationship tension with the mystery, action, or other plot. You must have some event occur on both sides, on the sexual tension side and on the mystery or action side to balance out the book.

Record and Transcribe Life Stories as Highlights, Turning Points, Skits, or Significant Events:

Recording and transcribing personal histories in their original form and/or as skits, plays, monologues, stories, novels, and memoirs are team projects of the person whose life is being turned into a time capsule and for the personal historian with a video camera, tape recorder, and notepad. For every action in a life story, there's an equal and opposite reaction that's primarily character-driven and secondarily plot-driven. And in an autobiography or anyone's life story, relationship tension occurs.

Then the plot moves on. You may not use the entire life history, but only highlights, events, experiences, and excerpts, stages of life and rites of passages.

If it's a romantic suspense or mystery within a life story, such as true confession, true crime, or biography, usually twenty-four short chapters makes a book-length story. Note how the memories are brought up by associations with various words, places, or questions.

A diary is written in first person as a journal or log, but a biography can be of you or your client. Even in a memoirs book or diary, you have to balance action with interaction between the heroine and the hero.

You can be the only person in your diary, but the action and interaction needs to be balanced with something out there in the external world—either forces of nature or another person—or the competition.

If you keep the competition out of your diary, put in the memories, actions, and warmth of the friends, including pets. If there are no other people, put in some force of spirit, some other push and pull, or tension, for balance with something outside yourself. This can be a job, school, a hobby, or what you choose as the force that pulls in an opposite direction existing with the force or person that pulls in your direction.

Try putting the relationship tension between the hero and heroine in the even-numbered chapters, and the mystery, historical events, or action plot events in the odd-numbered chapters.

In a 24-chapter—historical romance, this alternating action chapter, romantic tension chapter balances the plot smoothly. Most historical romance novels have 22-24 chapters. If you analyze the best-selling ones, you'll see that chapter one has an opening scene on the action side so you see what's happening.

The first action-oriented introductory chapter that shows us what's happening is followed by the second chapter on the romantic tension side showing us when and how the heroine meets the hero or has a re-union with the hero. In the second chapter, the writer takes the heroine somewhere in place or time. The heroine in the second chapter is defined. Either she's a 90's woman, or she's in her place in history or rebelling against it. You tell the story. If you're male, you'd use a hero.

Romantic life stories featuring genealogy combined with biography usually are 10-12 chapters long. Historical romances are twice that size at 22-24 chapters. The writer decides whether it's best to turn a biography into a historical romance or a life story into a mystery, suspense, action adventure, young adult novel, romance, or other genre.

If you are not fictionalizing genealogy or biography into a story, keep your time capsule book, database, or other media true to facts and historical records only. You might want to add your DNA testing records of relatives along with a family tree or other database or time capsule.

For those who want to turn factual biography into a novel, in turning a biography into a romance, the romantic tension side is about girl meeting hero in the first chapter. In the second chapter, the hero takes her somewhere in place, space, time, or state of mind. An oral history may be written as true life story in the form of a novel or play, skit, or anecdote of experience.

The oral history highlights a life experience within a time frame set in one or more locations with all the nuances of that place. It's basically a life story, but it can be transcribed with that certain something, including—charisma, liveliness, action, forward movement, drama, tension, and unique experiences, problems solved, and goals.

*   *   *

Writing Dialogue:

Here are examples of short story content that you can extract and revise in order to write short, concrete dialogue for a play. Don't write generalities or abstract ideas in your play. Explain everything in detail, factually. Don't write about theories. Instead, show examples of concrete specifics. Use the examples below to change from short story style into dialogue for a stage play or skit.

Notice the first half of the tome below is more concrete, and the last half is more abstract. As you revise into dialogue for a skit, play, or monologue, shorten the dialogue and make the words specific. Show examples. Don't bring abstract theories into dialogue for the stage.

Everything needs to be felt and experienced by the audience as they listen to the specific words and react to the details and examples. Below is a description with dialogue that in the second half turns into a monologue that is purposely more abstract. How will you pull the piece together and make it concrete so that you show in words instead of describe? Your goal is to show rather than tell.

Title: Techno-Stress
He slipped a software disc into the machine, impatient for the whirring computer to accept his commands, to be under his control. He tried to hurry it up. But the screen swirled into a spotty spin of confusion.
"Techno-stress. That's what we're suffering from, Eric. You expect me to respond to your orders like a computer. And when I don't, you lose your patience. Do you know why you're so insensitive to my feelings? Women are as interchangeable to you as computer peripherals."
He slammed the door, drowning but my shrill voice.
"Give me the right to tell you my feelings, Eric. I promise I won't accuse you anymore. Just accept the fact that I have feelings different from yours."
I stopped begging. "I can't ever get through to your passive-aggressive, withdrawing personality," I muttered. "It drives me wild!"
A moment later, now calm as if nothing happened, Eric called to my. "Come see my new modem."
"Why don't I go in my room and put on my computer?" I knew he was into his usual denial now. "Then your computer can talk to my computer the rest of the evening. Sounds like fun, eh?"
"Oh, it's going to run up the electricity bill," Eric complained.
"Come on. Just a few minutes. Then we'll play a board game. You like that, don't you?"
Eric hesitated. "Just five minutes. Then I have to work out my software program. I promised someone at work I'd volunteer take a bug out of the damn thing."
"Well, you're not getting paid for it."
I scampered like a child to my room and booted up Eric's other computer. I slipped aside a page from the new screenplay I'd been writing on it. "They don't make 'em like you, anymore, or like me," I said to my old, manual typewriter beside my desk.
The modem flashed red lights. Eric keyboarded on his computer, "I'm moving back to Maryland. I want a bigger house."

His message came up on my computer screen. As soon as he paused for my reply, I typed back, "What will become of me when I'm an old lady that everybody spits at?"

He paused and keyboarded, "We can get a house with a big yard real cheap back East, and I can walk in the woods to experience the change of seasons. I'm a cold-weather guy."

Then I typed back, "What if I slip and fall on the ice and break a hip in those snowy winters when I'm old with hollow bones? I'm a tropical fiesta person who loves the swaying palms and the long walks on the beaches at sunset. I demand Romance."

Eric read my message and entered in capital letters, "TAKE IT OR LEAVE IT. You don't slip and fall to break a hip. The hip gives way first from bone loss if you don't take your natural progesterone, and then you fall. I read all this in my holistic health books and magazines. If I'm good for something, it's guarding the money and nutrition of this household."

I smiled with predictability at Eric's ways. He seemed to grow on my after all those years of marriage. I needed to escape to my world, and so clicked on my television set. The bed was warm and soft. I rested against a mountain of pillows and shifted my remote control device until *The Apprentice* came on the screen. At last I was at peace.

Eric was in my room within five minutes to say goodnight as he had every evening. He opened the door without knocking and stood with slumped shoulders by my bedside.

"Stand up, if you want your good-night hug. I'm too tired to bend my aching back."

I jumped up not to miss my only chance to get five seconds of body contact. He gave me a brief, finger-tapping hug. Eric's head towered over mine by a foot. He was watching the television set, hypnotized by the flashing patterns.

"Don't you ever look at me when you hug me? Can't you rub my back smoothly instead of that nervous finger patting?"

"I can't be perfect. You're not my ideal, either."

"I'm sorry, Eric. That radio psychologist made me promise not to criticize you for not being a perfect prince."

"I promise next Saturday night I'll give you a hug. I've run out of gas."

"Next Saturday night will be another excuse, just like it always has been. I need my twelve hugs a day." I squirmed in his grip. As soon as he recognized my neediness, Eric danced away. I called him the take-away-man. Whatever he gave, he quickly took away something more valuable.

He peered on my desk and saw a file marked "Science Fiction."

"Ever notice how smart those who read and write science fiction are and how glamorous the romance writers are?"

"Not really."

Eric insisted. "Why don't you write romance?"

"Why don't you?"

"Men's brains are wired differently."

Eric hurried into his own room, sliding the deadbolt lock on his bedroom door. I climbed back under the covers and watched the rest of the television show.

Love had reeled down the most revolutionary road. At last I had taught myself to set limits. I wrote with the passion of a woman who faced my broken-ness, who had finally broadcasted in a loud voice: I want. I need.

No longer was I concealed from myself or the world. By five the next morning I was back at the computer writing my new "Woman in Space" series that would never see daylight outside my shelf, rejected too many times to count by those who count.

The blank page glared before my as I typed my opening lines: Right Brain-Left Brain Couples. Due to different ways of solving problems, he had a career in hard science. My career soared in poetry therapy.

I loved to work on many imaginative levels at one time. Poetry put me into a trance where I suspended my normal way of thinking. Every dream I had, every fear was a product of a conflict and my attempt to resolve it. I had become the character I hated most and loved most. And when I saw what I had done, I contested the origins, re-inventions, and recycling of my own identity. In the mystic, truth became concrete. In the abstract, intuition evolved into resource.

Yet—if I were to create wombs in men, caverns of deep, physical thinking, then I would risk life for one moment of absolute power. You see me in a pink mist, my face blurred by your anger and my fear of your anger. You gaze with those unfocused eyes that forever stare at a point above my shoulders. You taunt me with your wicked mouth and swing your brittle legs like fascists in pantyhose. I only seek to find all the universals in me that make sense to you. The search for identity is only one part of the whole universal shebang.

Men are what they are, I say. Women, by where their husbands itch, are judged at work by wives who marry rich. "And what does your father do" say young men before they dance. Will he set me up in business? Will he pay to take a chance?

The dusty years rolled by. These memoirs give me strength now that I can work for my next meal, twist through sieves, or tap a time capsule for nourishment.

Growing up means always having to revise. I, at last, remain, boss of my own creativity. So there really doesn't have to be opposites, after all. Who needs polarity when you can experience irony by observing? You can seek joy of life through metaphor. You can seek visual anthropology through journalism. Why be abstract when you can be concrete and write through and with the senses—including the sixth sense of intuition?

You can view life up close or remotely from an armchair. Why view when you can have insight, hindsight, and foresight? Why observe as a journalist, when you can read how to avoid the pitfalls from anthropologists—my role models?

You can reach the universal through the details. The person is the archetype, and the archetype is the person. The universal abstract is in the concrete reality. The future is in the present. The person who is shy isn't really shy. He's only taking a sudden interest in his toes. Play writing is all about living the design-driven life. And the design-driven life has a purpose: To inspire and motivate persistence.

***

Appendix A

Ethnic Genealogy Web Sites

Acadian/Cajun: & French Canadian: http://www.acadian.org/tidbits.html

African-American: http://www.cyndislist.com/african.htm

African Royalty Genealogy: http://www.uq.net.au/~zzhsoszy/

Albanian Research List: http://feefhs.org/al/alrl.html

Armenian Genealogical Society: http://feefhs.org/am/frg-amgs.html

Asia and the Pacific: http://www.cyndislist.com/asia.htm

Austria-Hungary Empire: http://feefhs.org/ah/indexah.html

Baltic-Russian Information Center: http://feefhs.org/blitz/frgblltz.html

Belarusian—Association of the Belarusian Nobility:
http://feefhs.org/by/frg-zbs.html

Bukovina Genealogy: http://feefhs.org/bukovina/bukovina.html

Carpatho-Rusyn Knowledge Base: http://feefhs.org/rusyn/frg-crkb.html

Chinese Genealogy: http://www.chineseroots.com.

Croatia Genealogy Cross Index: http://feefhs.org/cro/indexcro.html

Czechoslovak Genealogical Society Int'l, Inc.:
http://feefhs.org/czs/cgsi/frg-cgsi.html

Eastern Europe: http://www.cyndislist.com/easteuro.htm

Eastern European Genealogical Society, Inc.: http://feefhs.org/ca/frg-eegs.html

Eastern Europe Ethnic, Religious, and National Index with Home Pages includes the FEEFHS Resource Guide that lists organizations associated with FEEFHS from 14 Countries. It also includes Finnish and Armenian genealogy resources: http://feefhs.org/ethnic.html

Ethnic, Religious, and National Index 14 countries: http://feefhs.org/ethnic.html

Finnish Genealogy Group: http://feefhs.org/misc/frgfinmn.html

Galicia Jewish SIG: http://feefhs.org/jsig/frg-gsig.html

German Genealogical Digest: http://feefhs.org/pub/frg-ggdp.html

Greek Genealogy Sources on the Internet:
http://www-personal.umich.edu/~cgaunt/greece.html

Genealogy Societies Online List:
http://www.daddezio.com/catalog/grkndx04.html

German Research Association: http://feefhs.org/gra/frg-gra.html

Greek Genealogy (Hellenes-Diaspora Greek Genealogy):
http://www.geocities.com/SouthBeach/Cove/4537/

Greek Genealogy Home Page: http://www.daddezio.com/grekgen.html

Greek Genealogy Articles: http://www.daddezio.com/catalog/grkndx01.html

India Genealogy: http://genforum.genealogy.com/india/

India Family Histories:
http://www.mycinnamontoast.com/perl/results.cgi?region=79&sort=n

India-Anglo-Indian/Europeans in India genealogy:
http://members.ozemail.com.au/~clday/

Irish Travelers: http://www.pitt.edu/~alkst3/Traveller.html

Japanese Genealogy: http://www.rootsweb.com/~jpnwgw/

Jewish Genealogy: http://www.jewishgen.org/infofiles/

Latvian Jewish Genealogy Page: http://feefhs.org/jsig/frg-lsig.html

Lebanese Genealogy: http://www.rootsweb.com/~lbnwgw/

Lithuanian American Genealogy Society: http://feefhs.org/frg-lags.html

Melungeon: http://www.geocities.com/Paris/5121/melungeon.htm

Mennonite Heritage Center: http://feefhs.org/men/frg-mhc.html

Middle East Genealogy: http://www.rootsweb.com/~mdeastgw/index.html

Middle East Genealogy by country:
http://www.rootsweb.com/~mdeastgw/index.html#country

Native American: http://www.cyndislist.com/native.htm

Polish Genealogical Society of America: http://feefhs.org/pol/frg-pgsa.html

Quebec and Francophone: http://www.francogene.com/quebec/amerin.html

Romanian American Heritage Center: http://feefhs.org/ro/frg-rahc.html

Slovak World: http://feefhs.org/slovak/frg-sw.html

Slavs, South: Cultural Society: http://feefhs.org/frg-csss.html

Syrian and Lebanese Genealogy: http://www.genealogytoday.com/family/syrian/

Syria Genealogy: http://www.rootsweb.com/~syrwgw/

Tibetan Genealogy:
http://www.distantcousin.com/Links/Ethnic/China/Tibetan.html

Turkish Genealogy Discussion Group:
http://www.turkey.com/forums/forumdisplay.php3?forumid=18

Ukrainian Genealogical and Historical Society of Canada:
http://feefhs.org/ca/frgughsc.html

Unique Peoples: http://www.cyndislist.com/peoples.htm Note: The Unique People's list includes: **Black Dutch**, **Doukhobors**, **Gypsy, Romani, Romany & Travellers**, **Melungeons**, **Metis**, **Miscellaneous**, and **Wends/Sorbs**

Appendix B

Genealogy Web sites, (General)

Ancestry.com: http://www.ancestry.com/main.htm?lfl=m

Cyndi's List of Genealogy on the Internet: http://www.cyndislist.com/

Cyndi's List is a categorized & cross-referenced index to genealogical resources on the Internet with thousands of links.

DistantCousin.com (Uniting Cousins Worldwide)
http://distantcousin.com/Links/surname.html

Ellis Island Online: http://www.ellisisland.org/

Family History Library: http://www.familysearch.org/Eng/default.asp

http://www.familysearch.org/Eng/Search/frameset_search.asp

(The Church of Jesus Christ of Latter Day Saints) International Genealogical Index

Female Ancestors: http://www.cyndislist.com/female.htm

Genealogist's Index to the Web: http://www.genealogytoday.com/GIWWW/?

Genealogy Web http://www.genealogyweb.com/

Genealogy Authors and Speakers: http://feefhs.org/frg/frg-a&l.html

Genealogy Today: http://www.genealogytoday.com/

My Genealogy.com http://www.genealogy.com/cgi-bin/my_main.cgi

Scriver, Dr. Charles: The Canadian Medical Hall of Fame
http://www.virtualmuseum.ca/Exhibitions/Medicentre/en/scri_print.htm

Surname Sites: http://www.cyndislist.com/surn-gen.htm

National Genealogical Society: http://www.ngsgenealogy.org/index.htm

United States List of Local by State Genealogical Societies:
http://www.daddezio.com/society/hill/index.html

United States Vital Records List:
http://www.daddezio.com/records/room/index.html or
http://www.cyndislist.com/usvital.htm

Appendix C

1,004 Action Verbs for Communicators

1) Abated
2) Abbreviated
3) Abstracted
4) Abided
5) Abjured
6) Abnegated
7) Abraded
8) Abridged
9) Abrogated
10) Abseiled
11) Absolved
12) Abstained
13) Absorbed
14) Abstracted
15) Abutted
16) Accelerated
17) Accented
18) Accentuated
19) Accepted
20) Acclaimed
21) Acclimatized

22) Accommodated
23) Accompanied
24) Accomplished
25) Accorded
26) Accounted
27) Accredited
28) Accrued
29) Accumulated
30) Accustomed
31) Achieved
32) Acknowledged
33) Acquainted
34) Acquiesced
35) Acquired
36) Acquitted
37) Acted
38) Activated
39) Actualized
40) Actuated
41) Adapted
42) Added

43) Addressed
44) Adduced
45) Adhered
46) Adjudged
47) Adjudicated
48) Adjoined
49) Adjourned
50) Adjured
51) Adjusted
52) Ad-libbed
53) Administered
54) Admired
55) Admitted
56) Adopted
57) Adored
58) Adorned
59) Adumbrated
60) Advanced
61) Advertised
62) Advised
63) Advocated
64) Aerated
65) Affected
66) Affiliated
67) Affirmed
68) Affixed
69) Afforded
70) Agglutinated
71) Aggrandized
72) Agreed
73) Aided
74) Aligned
75) Allied
76) Allocated
77) Allotted
78) Alternated

79) Amazed
80) Amended
81) Amplified
82) Amused
83) Analyzed
84) Anesthetized
85) Animated
86) Annotated
87) Announced
88) Answered
89) Anticipated
90) Appealed
91) Appeared
92) Appended
93) Appertained (to)
94) Applauded
95) Applied
96) Appliquéd
97) Appointed
98) Appraised
99) Apprised
100) Approached
101) Approved
102) Approximated
103) Arbitrated
104) Archived
105) Argued
106) Arose (from)
107) Arranged
108) Arrived
109) Articulated
110) Ascertained
111) Ascribed
112) Aspired
113) Assayed
114) Assembled

115) Asserted	151) Bought
116) Assessed	152) Braided
117) Assigned	153) Brailed
118) Assimilated	154) Branched
119) Assisted	155) Brandished
120) Associated	156) Branded
121) Assumed	157) Bred
122) Assured	158) Breaded
123) Astonished	159) Broadcasted
124) Astounded	160) Brought
125) Attached	161) Budgeted
126) Attained	162) Built
127) Attempted	163) Calculated
128) Attended	164) Calmed
129) Attitudinized	165) Campaigned
130) Attributed	166) Camped
131) Attuned	167) Captivated
132) Audited	168) Carded
133) Audiodidacted	169) Cared
134) Audio taped	170) Carried
135) Augmented	171) Carted
136) Authored	172) Carved
137) Authorize	173) Catalogued
138) Automated	174) Catapulted
139) Availed	175) Centered
140) Awarded	176) Chaired
141) Became	177) Changed
142) Backed	178) Channeled
143) Banked	179) Characterized
144) Banded	180) Charged
145) Bartered	181) Charted
146) Beaded	182) Chartered
147) Begot	183) Cheered
148) Benchmarked	184) Cherished
149) Benefited	185) Chiseled
150) Booked	186) Chronicled

187)	Cited	223)	Conducted
188)	Civilized	224)	Configured
189)	Claimed	225)	Congratulated
190)	Clarified	226)	Congregated
191)	Cleaned	227)	Connected
192)	Cleared	228)	Connoted
193)	Clocked	229)	Conquered
194)	Closed	230)	Conserved
195)	Clued	231)	Considered
196)	Coached	232)	Constructed
197)	Coded	233)	Construed
198)	Codified	234)	Consulted
199)	Coifed	235)	Consumed
200)	Collaborated	236)	Contracted
201)	Collected	237)	Continued
202)	Colored	238)	Contributed
203)	Comforted	239)	Controlled
204)	Commanded	240)	Converged
205)	Commemorated	241)	Conversed
206)	Commercialized	242)	Cooperated
207)	Commissioned	243)	Co-opted
208)	Communicated	244)	Coordinated
209)	Compared	245)	Copyrighted
210)	Compensated	246)	Corded
211)	Competed	247)	Corrected
212)	Compiled	248)	Correlated
213)	Complimented	249)	Counseled
214)	Completed	250)	Counted
215)	Composed	251)	Countered
216)	Computed	252)	Courted
217)	Computerized	253)	Created
218)	Conceived	254)	Credited
219)	Concentrated	255)	Crewed
220)	Conceptualized	256)	Critiqued
221)	Conciliated	257)	Crusaded
222)	Concluded	258)	Cued

259)	Cultured	295)	Described
260)	Curtailed	296)	Designed
261)	Customized	297)	Detailed
262)	Cut	298)	Detected
263)	Cycled	299)	Determined
264)	Dated	300)	Detoured
265)	Dealt	301)	Developed
266)	Debited	302)	Devised
267)	Debriefed	303)	Devolved
268)	Debugged	304)	Dined
269)	Detailed	305)	Disclosed
270)	Decentralized	306)	Divided
271)	Decided	307)	Divulged
272)	Deciphered	308)	Delighted
273)	Declaimed	309)	Derived
274)	Declared	310)	Devised
275)	Decoded	311)	Devoted
276)	Decorated	312)	Diagnosed
277)	Decreased	313)	Dialogued
278)	Dedicated	314)	Diced
279)	Deferred	315)	Dichotomized
280)	Defined	316)	Dictated
281)	Deflected	317)	Differed
282)	Delegated	318)	Digested
283)	Deleted	319)	Digitized
284)	Delighted (in)	320)	Dignified
285)	Delineated	321)	Diluted
286)	Delivered	322)	Directed
287)	Demonstrated	323)	Digitized
288)	Demystified	324)	Disagreed
289)	Denominate	325)	Disclosed
290)	Denoted	326)	Discovered
291)	Depicted	327)	Discussed
292)	Deprogrammed	328)	Dispatched
293)	Deregulated	329)	Dispersed
294)	Derived	330)	Displayed

331) Dissolved
332) Distributed
333) Diversified
334) Divided
335) Divined
336) Documented
337) Docked
338) Donated
339) Doused
340) Drafted
341) Drew
342) Drove
343) Earned
344) Edited
345) Editorialized
346) Educated
347) Effected
348) Effloresced
349) Eked out
350) Elaborated
351) Elasticized
352) Elbowed
353) Elected
354) Elegized
355) Elevated
356) Eliminated
357) Embroidered
358) Emended
359) Emphasized
360) Employed
361) Empowered
362) Encased
363) Encountered
364) Encouraged
365) Energized
366) Engaged

367) Engineered
368) Engraved
369) Enhanced
370) Enlarged
371) Enlightened
372) Enlisted
373) Enlivened
374) Enriched
375) Ensured
376) Entered
377) Entertained
378) Envisioned
379) Epigrammatized
380) Epitomized
381) Equalized
382) Erected
383) Eructed
384) Escorted
385) Established
386) Estimated
387) Etched
388) Etiolated
389) Eulogized
390) Euphemized
391) Evaluated
392) Evanesced
393) Evangelized
394) Evidenced
395) Evoked
396) Evolved
397) Exacerbated
398) Exacted
399) Exalted
400) Examined
401) Excavated
402) Excelled

403)	Exchanged	439)	Filed
404)	Exclaimed	440)	Filled
405)	Excoriated	441)	Filmed
406)	Exculpated	442)	Financed
407)	Executed	443)	Fired
408)	Exemplified	444)	Fitted
409)	Exercised	445)	Fixed
410)	Exhorted	446)	Flattered
411)	Exfoliated	447)	Flew
412)	Exhibited	448)	Flaunted
413)	Exonerated	449)	Flourished
414)	Exorcized	450)	Fluctuated
415)	Expanded	451)	Flummoxed
416)	Expatiated	452)	Followed
417)	Expedited	453)	Forecasted
418)	Experienced	454)	Formalized
419)	Explained	455)	Formatted
420)	Explored	456)	Formed
421)	Exported	457)	Formulated
422)	Exposed	458)	Fortified
423)	Expressed	459)	Forwarded
424)	Extended	460)	Found
425)	Extolled	461)	Founded
426)	Extrapolated	462)	Franchised
427)	Facilitated	463)	Fraternized
428)	Farmed	464)	Freed
429)	Fascinated	465)	Froze
430)	Fastened	466)	Fulfilled
431)	Faxed	467)	Functioned
432)	Fed	468)	Furnished
433)	Federalized	469)	Gained
434)	Felicitated	470)	Garnished
435)	Ferreted	471)	Gathered
436)	Fertilized	472)	Gave
437)	Fetched	473)	Generated
438)	Fictionalized	474)	Genealogized

475)	Geneticized	511)	Hosted
476)	Genuflected	512)	Hugged
477)	Gestured	513)	Humanized
478)	Gesticulated	514)	Humored
479)	Girded	515)	Hustled
480)	Glorified	516)	Hypnotized
481)	Gnosticized	517)	Hypothesized
482)	Governed	518)	Identified
483)	Graded	519)	Ignited
484)	Grafted	520)	Illustrated
485)	Granted	521)	Immigrated
486)	Graphed	522)	Implanted
487)	Gratified	523)	Implemented
488)	Greeted	524)	Implied
489)	Grew	525)	Imported
490)	Guaranteed	526)	Imposed
491)	Guarded	527)	Impressed
492)	Guided	528)	Improved
493)	Hafted	529)	Incited
494)	Hailed	530)	Included
495)	Halted	531)	Incorporated
496)	Handled	532)	Increased
497)	Harbored	533)	Indexed
498)	Harmonized	534)	Indicated
499)	Hastened	535)	Indicted
500)	Harvested	536)	Indulged
501)	Headed	537)	Industrialized
502)	Healed	538)	Influenced
503)	Heaped	539)	Informed
504)	Heard	540)	Initialized
505)	Heated	541)	Initiated
506)	Helped	542)	Inked
507)	Hewed	543)	Inquired
508)	Hired	544)	Inspected
509)	Honored	545)	Inspired
510)	Hoped	546)	Installed

547)	Instituted	583)	Legalized
548)	Instructed	584)	Legitimized
549)	Insured	585)	Legislated
550)	Integrated	586)	Lessened
551)	Interested	587)	Led
552)	Interfaced	588)	Left
553)	Internalized	589)	Lighted
554)	Internationalized	590)	Linked
555)	Interpreted	591)	Listened
556)	Interviewed	592)	Litigated
557)	Introduced	593)	Loaded
558)	Intuited	594)	Loaned
559)	Invested	595)	Lobbied
560)	Investigated	596)	Localized
561)	Invented	597)	Looked
562)	Inventoried	598)	Lyricized
563)	Inverted	599)	Magnetized
564)	Invested	600)	Mailed
565)	Invigorated	601)	Maintained
566)	Involved	602)	Managed
567)	Issued	603)	Manipulated
568)	Joined	604)	Manufactured
569)	Journalized	605)	Marked
570)	Journeyed	606)	Marketed
571)	Judged	607)	Mastered
572)	Juried	608)	Measured
573)	Justified	609)	Mediated
574)	Juxtaposed	610)	Memorized
575)	Keyboarded	611)	Mentored
576)	Lamented	612)	Merchandised
577)	Laminated	613)	Merged
578)	Landed (in)	614)	Met
579)	Landscaped	615)	Micrographed
580)	Leased	616)	Migrated
581)	Launched	617)	Ministered
582)	Lectured	618)	Moderated

619)	Modified		655)	Outlined
620)	Modeled		656)	Outnumbered
621)	Molded		657)	Outpaced
622)	Monitored		658)	Outperformed
623)	Morphed		659)	Outplayed
624)	Mortgaged		660)	Outran
625)	Motivated		661)	Outshone
626)	Moved		662)	Outranked
627)	Multiplied		663)	Outvoted
628)	Multitasked		664)	Outwitted
629)	Narrated		665)	Overawed
630)	Navigated		666)	Overcame
631)	Negotiated		667)	Overdid
632)	Networked		668)	Overheard
633)	Neutered		669)	Oversaw
634)	Neutralized		670)	Overstepped
635)	Normalized		671)	Overstretched
636)	Normed		672)	Overwhelmed
637)	Notated		673)	Overworked
638)	Noted		674)	Overwrote
639)	Notified		675)	Owed
640)	Notarized		676)	Owned
641)	Nourished		677)	Oxygenated
642)	Nursed		678)	Oxidized
643)	Obtained		679)	Paced
644)	Officiated		680)	Packaged
645)	Opened		681)	Packed
646)	Orated		682)	Parented
647)	Operated		683)	Participated
648)	Opined		684)	Partnered (with)
649)	Orchestrated		685)	Patented
650)	Ordered		686)	Patterned
651)	Organized		687)	Perceived
652)	Oriented		688)	Perfected
653)	Originated		689)	Performed
654)	Outlaid		690)	Persevered

691)	Persisted	727)	Produced
692)	Personalized	728)	Professionalized
693)	Persuaded	729)	Programmed
694)	Perused	730)	Projected
695)	Petitioned	731)	Promulgated
696)	Photocopied	732)	Promoted
697)	Photographed	733)	Proposed
698)	Piloted	734)	Proscribed
699)	Pinpointed	735)	Proofread
700)	Pitched	736)	Prospered
701)	Placed	737)	Protected
702)	Planned	738)	Protested
703)	Planted	739)	Protracted
704)	Played	740)	Proved
705)	Plotted	741)	Provided
706)	Pooled	742)	Publicized
707)	Posed	743)	Published
708)	Posted	744)	Purchased
709)	Positioned	745)	Pursued
710)	Practiced	746)	Qualified
711)	Praised	747)	Quantified
712)	Prayed	748)	Quickened
713)	Predicted	749)	Questioned
714)	Preempted	750)	Queued
715)	Prefaced	751)	Quilted
716)	Preferred	752)	Raised
717)	Prepared	753)	Ran
718)	Presented	754)	Ranged
719)	Presided	755)	Rated
720)	Pressed	756)	Razed
721)	Prevented	757)	Reached
722)	Probed	758)	Realized
723)	Proceeded (to)	759)	Reaped
724)	Processed	760)	Rearranged
725)	Procreated	761)	Reared
726)	Procured	762)	Reasoned

763) Recalled
764) Recited
765) Received
766) Recited
767) Reclaimed
768) Recognized
769) Recommended
770) Reconciled
771) Reconstructed
772) Recorded
773) Recouped
774) Recovered
775) Recreated
776) Recruited
777) Rectified
778) Recycled
779) Redesigned
780) Redecorated
781) Redistricted
782) Reduced
783) Reenacted
784) Reentered
785) Referenced
786) Refreshed
787) Registered
788) Regulated
789) Rehearsed
790) Rehired
791) Reimbursed
792) Reinforced
793) Rejoiced
794) Related
795) Released
796) Relinquished
797) Relocated
798) Remedied

799) Reminisced
800) Remembered
801) Remodeled
802) Renewed
803) Rented
804) Reoriented
805) Repaired
806) Replenished
807) Replied
808) Reported
809) Reposed
810) Represented
811) Requested
812) Required
813) Requisitioned
814) Researched
815) Resized
816) Reshaped
817) Resolved
818) Respected
819) Responded to
820) Restored
821) Resourced
822) Resulted
823) Retailed
824) Retained
825) Retrained
826) Retired
827) Retooled
828) Retorted
829) Retrained
830) Retrieved
831) Returned
832) Reunited
833) Revamped
834) Reveled

835) Reviewed	871) Skilled
836) Revised	872) Socialized
837) Revived	873) Sold
838) Rewired	874) Solicited
839) Roboticized	875) Solidified
840) Rolled	876) Solved
841) Rose	877) Sorted
842) Rotated	878) Sought
843) Routed	879) Spared
844) Rushed	880) Sparked
845) Sailed	881) Spayed
846) Sampled	882) Specified
847) Sanitized	883) Speculated
848) Saved	884) Spiced
849) Scanned	885) Spirited
850) Scheduled	886) Spoke
851) Scored	887) Sponsored
852) Screened	888) Spread
853) Scrimped	889) Staffed
854) Sculptured	890) Stabilized
855) Secured	891) Standardized
856) Sequenced	892) Starred
857) Selected	893) Stated
858) Sensed	894) Stepped
859) Serialized	895) Sterilized
860) Served	896) Stimulated
861) Set objectives	897) Stored
862) Set up	898) Straightened
863) Sewed	899) Streamlined
864) Shaped	900) Strengthened
865) Shared	901) Stretched
866) Shredded	902) Strolled
867) Showed	903) Strove
868) Signified	904) Structured
869) Simplified	905) Styled
870) Sized	906) Subcontracted

907)	Submitted		943)	Translated
908)	Succeeded		944)	Transmitted
909)	Summarized		945)	Transported
910)	Supervised		946)	Traveled
911)	Supplied		947)	Treated
912)	Supported		948)	Trekked
913)	Surfed		949)	Triumphed
914)	Surmised		950)	Troubleshot
915)	Surveyed		951)	Trucked
916)	Survived		952)	Truncated
917)	Syndicated		953)	Trusted
918)	Synthesized		954)	Turned
919)	Systematized		955)	Typed
920)	Tabulated		956)	Typeset
921)	Tamped		957)	Understood
922)	Taught		958)	Undertook
923)	Taxed		959)	Unified
924)	Teamed (up)		960)	United
925)	Telecommuted		961)	Updated
926)	Telemarketed		962)	Upgraded
927)	Telephoned		963)	Uplifted
928)	Televised		964)	Underscored
929)	Terminated		965)	Used
930)	Tested		966)	Utilized
931)	Thwarted		967)	Validated
932)	Told		968)	Valued
933)	Tolled		969)	Varied
934)	Toughened		970)	Vaunted
935)	Toured		971)	Venerated
936)	Traced		972)	Ventured
937)	Tracked		973)	Verbalized
938)	Traded		974)	Verified
939)	Trained		975)	Videotaped
940)	Transacted		976)	Viewed
941)	Transcribed		977)	Vindicated
941)	Transferred		978)	Visualized

979) Vitalized
980) Vocalized
981) Voiced
982) Volunteered
983) Voted
984) Vulcanized
985) Waited
986) Waived
987) Watched
988) Waved
989) Weaned
990) Weighed
991) Weighted
992) Welded
993) Willed
994) Wintered
995) Withdrew
996) Wholesaled
997) Won
998) Word processed
999) Worked
1000) Wrote
1001) Yearned
1002) Yielded
1003) Zeroed
1004) Zoned

Appendix D

List of Published Paperback Books in Print Written by Anne Hart

1. Title: How to Interpret Family History and Ancestry DNA Test Results for Beginners: The Geography and History of Your Relatives
ISBN: 0-595-31684-0

2. Title: Cover Letters, Follow-Ups, and Book Proposals: Samples with Templates
ISBN: 0-595-31663-8

3. Title: Writer's Guide to Book Proposals: Templates, Query Letters, & Free Media Publicity
ISBN: 0-595-31673-5

4. Title: Title: Search Your Middle Eastern & European Genealogy: In the Former Ottoman Empire's Records and Online
ISBN:0-595-31811-8

5. Title: Is Radical Liberalism or Extreme Conservatism a Character Disorder, Mental Disease, or Publicity Campaign?—A Novel of Intrigue—
ISBN: 0-595-31751-0

6. Title: Action Verbs for Communicators
ISBN: 0-595-31911-4

7. Title: How to Make Money Organizing Information
ISBN: 0-595-23695-2

8. Title: How To Stop Elderly Abuse: A Prevention Guidebook
ISBN: 0-595-23550-6

9. Title: How to Make Money Teaching Online With Your Camcorder and PC: 25 Practical and Creative How-To Start-Ups To Teach Online
ISBN: 0-595-22123-8

10. Title: A Private Eye Called Mama Africa: What's an Egyptian Jewish Female Psycho-Sleuth Doing Fighting Hate Crimes in California?
ISBN: 0-595-18940-7

11. Title: The Freelance Writer's E-Publishing Guidebook: 25+ E-Publishing Home-based Online Writing Businesses to Start for Freelancers
ISBN: 0-595-18952-0

12. Title: The Courage to Be Jewish and the Wife of an Arab Sheik: What's a Jewish Girl from Brooklyn Doing Living as a Bedouin?
ISBN: 0-595-18790-0

13. Title: The Year My Whole Country Turned Jewish: A Time-Travel Adventure Novel in Medieval Khazaria
ISBN: 0-75967-251-2

14. Stage Play Book: ISBN:

15. Title: The Day My Whole Country Turned Jewish: The Silk Road Kids
ISBN: 0-7596-6380-7

16. Title: Four Astronauts and a Kitten: A Mother and Daughter Astronaut Team, the Teen Twin Sons, and Patches, the Kitten: The Intergalactic Friendship Club
ISBN: 0-595-19202-5

17. Title: The Writer's Bible: Digital and Print Media: Skills, Promotion, and Marketing for Novelists, Playwrights, and Script Writers. Writing Entertainment Content for the New and Print Media.
ISBN: 0-595-19305-6

18. Title: New Afghanistan's TV Anchorwoman: A novel of mystery set in the New Afghanistan
ISBN: 0-595-21557-2

19. Title: Tools for Mystery Writers: Writing Suspense Using Hidden Personality Traits
ISBN: 0-595-21747-8

20. Title: The Khazars Will Rise Again!: Mystery Tales of the Khazars
ISBN: 0-595-21830-X

21. Title: Murder in the Women's Studies Department: A Professor Sleuth Novel of Mystery
ISBN: 0-595-21859-8

22. Title: Make Money With Your Camcorder and PC: 25+ Businesses: Make Money With Your Camcorder and Your Personal Computer by Linking Them.
ISBN: 0-595-21864-4

23. Title: Writing What People Buy: 101+ Projects That Get Results
ISBN: 0-595-21936-5

24. Title: Anne Joan Levine, Private Eye: Internal adventure through first-person mystery writer's diary novels
ISBN: 0-595-21860-1

25. Title: Verbal Intercourse: A Darkly Humorous Novel of Interpersonal Couples and Family Communication
ISBN: 0-595-21946-2

26. Title: The Date Who Unleashed Hell: If You Love Me, Why Do You Humiliate Me?
"The Date" Mystery Fiction Series
ISBN: 0-595-21982-9

27. Title: Cleopatra's Daughter: Global Intercourse
ISBN: 0-595-22021-5

28. Title: Cyber Snoop Nation: The Adventures Of Littanie Webster, Sixteen-Year-Old Genius Private Eye On Internet Radio
ISBN: 0-595-22033-9

29. Title: Counseling Anarchists: We All Marry Our Mirrors—Someone Who Reflects How We Feel About Ourselves. Folding Inside Ourselves: A Novel of Mystery
ISBN: 0-595-22054-1

30. Title: Sacramento Latina: When the One Universal We Have In Common Divides Us
ISBN: 0-595-22061-4

31. Title: Astronauts and Their Cats: At night, the space station is cat-shadow dark
ISBN: 0-595-22330-3

32. Title: How Two Yellow Labs Saved the Space Program: When Smart Dogs Shape Shift in Space
ISBN: 0-595-23181-0

33. Title: The DNA Detectives: Working Against Time
ISBN: 0-595-25339-3

34. Title: How to Interpret Your DNA Test Results For Family History & Ancestry: Scientists Speak Out on Genealogy Joining Genetics
ISBN: 0-595-26334-8

35. Title: Roman Justice: SPQR: Too Roman To Handle
ISBN: 0-595-27282-7

36. Title: How to Make Money Selling Facts: to Non-Traditional Markets
ISBN: 0-595-27842-6

37. Title: Tracing Your Jewish DNA For Family History & Ancestry: Merging a Mosaic of Communities
ISBN: 0-595-28127-3

38. Title: The Beginner's Guide to Interpreting Ethnic DNA Origins for Family History: How Ashkenazi, Sephardi, Mizrahi & Europeans Are Related to Everyone Else
ISBN: 0-595-28306-3

39. Title: Nutritional Genomics—A Consumer's Guide to How Your Genes and Ancestry Respond to Food: Tailoring What You Eat to Your DNA
ISBN: 0-595-29067-1

40. Title: How to Safely Tailor Your Food, Medicines, & Cosmetics to Your Genes: A Consumer's Guide to Genetic Testing Kits from Ancestry to Nourishment
ISBN: 0-595-29403-0

41. Title: One Day Some Schlemiel Will Marry Me, Pay the Bills, and Hug Me.: Parents & Children Kvetch on Arab & Jewish Intermarriage
ISBN: 0-595-29826-5

42. Title: Find Your Personal Adam And Eve: Make DNA-Driven Genealogy Time Capsules
ISBN: 0-595-30633-0

43. Title: Creative Genealogy Projects: Writing Salable Life Stories
ISBN: 0-595-31305-1

44. Title: Power Dating Games: What's Important to Know About the Person You'll Marry
ISBN: 0-595-19186-X

45. Search Your Middle Eastern and European Genealogy: In the Former Ottoman Empire's Records and Online
ISBN: 0-595-31811-8

46. Ancient and Medieval Teenage Diaries:
ISBN: 0-595-32009-0

47. Dramatizing 17th Century Family History of Deacon Stephen Hart & Other Early New England Settlers
IBSN 0-595-34345-7

48. Problem-Solving & Cat Tales for the Holidays
ISBN: 0-595-32692-7

49. Cutting Expenses & Getting More for Less 41+ Ways to Earn an Income from Opportune Living
IBSN 0-595-34772-X

50. Writing 45-Minute One-Act Plays, Skits, Monologues, & Animation Scripts for Drama Workshops
IBSN 0-595-34597-2

Index

0-595-34597-2